CATHOLIC PRIMARY EDUCATION

Edited by Eugene Duffy

Catholic Primary Education: Facing New Challenges

the columba press

First published in 2012 by
the columba press
55A Spruce Avenue, Stillorgan Industrial Park,
Blackrock, Co Dublin

Cover by Bill Bolger
Origination by The Columba Press
Printed in Ireland by Gemini International Ltd, Dublin

ISBN 978 1 85607 7705

Contents

INTRODUCTION

Catholic Primary Education: Facing New Challenges

Catholic primary schools have been an integral part of parish life in Ireland for long over one hundred years and have been maintained with relative stability through significant social and political change. However, in the past few years their role and identity have been more critically questioned than at any time since the nineteenth century. There are approximately 3,400 primary schools in the country, comprising 92 per cent of educational provision at that level, serving about 1,360 parishes. These are remarkable figures by international standards. The economic boom that occurred from the late 1990s until recently saw a real change in the demographic make-up of the country. New immigrants from Eastern Europe, Africa and Asia have changed the racial, ethnic and religious profile of most schools in the country. Over the same period levels of participation in church life have declined dramatically, so that the role the parish schools previously played in supporting parents in the faith formation of their children can no longer be assumed to be operative in all cases. The demands of business and industry are responded to more immediately now than in the past, so that a more utilitarian or instrumentalist view of education is beginning to take hold. Such an approach is a serious challenge to the Catholic view of education, one that is much more holistic and more open to the development of a child's spiritual and moral development. Finally, some political agendas are seeking to determine a less majoritarian role for the Catholic Church in educational provision, a view not necessarily shared by all citizens. It is against the background of these considerations that the current collection of essays is being offered.

In response to some of these societal changes, the Minister of Education and Skills, Mr Ruairi Quinn, established a Forum on

Patronage and Pluralism, in April 2011, to prepare a report on primary school patronage with a view to establishing how and where it aught to be possible to create greater diversity in primary school provision. He deemed this important because the vast majority of all primary schools in the State are under Catholic patronage, which is an anomalous situation given the demographic profile of the primary school population. However, as the research carried out by the Catholic Schools Partnership has pointed out, patronage is not a concept widely understood by parents: ethos and the teaching of religious education are identified as the defining elements of the Church's involvement in primary education. This is but one example of the complexity facing anyone attempting to understand or to reform the current situation. The reality of faith-based schools is multi-faceted and there is no single issue, which if addressed, will provide an easy or neat solution to the perceived problems of the moment.

The Irish Episcopal Conference, also recognising the complexity of the current situation, issued a joint pastoral in May 2008, entitled *Vision 08*, in which the bishops set out their vision for Catholic education in Ireland into the future. In the opening paragraph of that document they acknowledged that the role of the Church in education has become an issue of intense debate, North and South, especially because of the growing cultural and religious pluralism on the island. Some of these issues made national headlines over the past few years as Catholic primary schools in the greater Dublin area were unable to cope with the numbers of children seeking enrolment and criteria for admission came under scrutiny. At the same time there are many primary schools in rural parts of the country with significant numbers of non-Christian pupils, thus presenting new challenges to teachers, pastoral carerers and boards of management. In Northern Ireland the issue of denominational education has been regularly debated over the past forty years. Debate, too, has been taking place around the role of the Churches in education in Britain and France in recent years as the wider debate about the place and role of religion in public life has resurfaced with fresh intensity. Although secularisation may appear to be the dominant mood, religion and its concerns have proven to be remarkably resilient.

Since the foundation of the State the Churches and various religious congregations have played an enormously significant role in the field of education as teachers, principals, managers and trustees of our schools, often making huge financial investments in the enterprise. Over several decades there has been a gradual and almost imperceptible change going on here, so that now there are very few religious personnel involved directly in the day to day life of schools.

In the past there were so many clergy and religious involved in educational provision that they and others could assume that they were indeed providing a Catholic education for their pupils. For the most part, what was meant by a Catholic education did not have to be spelled out in any great detail. A quick look at the school environment and the timetable would soon inform you of the fact that you were in a Catholic school. Most of the teaching staff, too, were committed to their faith and, like the majority of other members of the Church, were largely unquestioning of its authority.

We are now in an entirely different situation and it has become more urgent for the Church to spell out more precisely what it means to be a Catholic school. The old assumptions no longer hold. The case for a Catholic school, or indeed any denominational school, has to be more persuasively made. This is what the bishops were doing in their brief pastoral letter in 2008. In fact, their pastoral may be seen as an initial contribution to this task, as it ends with an invitation to begin a wider conversation among all the partners in education, so that the role of the Catholic school might be better articulated and understood.

This debate about the future of Catholic education in Ireland is an important one for both Church and society. On the one hand, the Church and its educational mission cannot be merged uncritically into the dominant agendas of the wider society. On the other hand, it cannot attempt to create an enclave that insulates itself from society and thus become a sectarian enterprise. It needs to be able to articulate what is its distinctive contribution to education and the common good. The argument has to be made as to why it deserves its place in the educational enterprise. A genuinely Catholic education can never deny the person an opportunity to explore what is genuinely human, whether the issue is discussed by the humanities or the hard sciences. Neither can it deny the person an opportunity to explore issues of meaning and value, faith and conviction. A genuinely tolerant society will see the value of supporting such an exploration as it will allow all of its members to enhance their own self-understanding and their understanding of their fellow citizens.

As a response to the invitation issued by the bishops in their pastoral letter, *Vision 08*, the McAuley Conference held at Mary Immaculate College, University of Limerick, in May 2009 addressed the issue of 'Catholic Primary Education: Facing New Horizons'. The current collection of essays represents some of the papers presented at the Conference as well as a number of others that have been specially commissioned for this volume. The essays here do not propose to cover all of the issues that are currently being debated in the public forum. Nevertheless, they do address some of the key issues that have to be considered by anyone who wishes to be informed about the provision of primary education within a faith-based context.

The topics covered include some broad discussion about the very nature of education and the challenges it faces in a society so preoccupied by economics and technology and in danger of losing sight of its more deeply rooted values of truth, freedom and empathy. This is followed by an exploration of the rationale for the Church's involvement in educational provision, especially in the light of its official teaching. This is further amplified by an exploration of the nature of, and challenges to, the Catholic Primary School in twenty-first century Ireland, taking into account current Irish and European legislation and directives in this area. In order to give further context to the reflections, a brief history of the Church's involvement in primary education in Ireland is provided, as well as two points of comparison, one from Australia and the other from Scotland. There are then two reflections on the perspectives of patrons and managers on primary school provision, examining some of the more specific legislative and administrative issues in these domains. A parent then reflects on her personal experience of being involved with the primary educational system, showing the unexpected consequences for her and her family. Finally, the collection ends with a review of what it means for a school to be a learning community, contributing to the formation of a learning society.

As this volume goes to print, the report from the Forum on Patronage and Pluralism is still awaited. Its findings will inevitably evoke further discussion of the role of the Catholic Church in the provision of primary education. Meanwhile, it is hoped that the essays in this volume will make a helpful contribution to the ensuing debate and draw attention to important values and perspectives that have to be borne in mind as we reimagine and reconfigure the role played by Catholic primary schools in a country undergoing significant social and religious transformation.

Eugene Duffy

CHAPTER ONE

Educate that you may be free? Religion and Critical Thinking in Post-Boom Ireland

Michael Cronin

If you happened to find yourself in Prague on the St. Patrick's Day 1977 and you went looking for flowers you might eventually ask yourself the following question. Why were all the florists closed? The answer was one man, the philosopher, Jan Patočka, alone responsible for this sudden dearth of flowers in the Czech capital. A founding signatory of Charter 77, he was repeatedly harassed by the state secret police. At the end of one particularly harrowing interrogation session, he died of apoplexy, aged sixty-nine. Determined that there should be no public display of support for the deceased thinker and activist, the authorities decreed that all flower shops remain closed on the day of his funeral. When the funeral orations began the police started revving up their motorcycle engines and a helicopter hovered low over the open grave. Five days before the interrogation session that cost him his life, Patočka wrote the following words in what was to be his last text:

> Let's be honest, in the past, conformism has never led to an improvement but a worsening of the situation [...] What is necessary is to behave at all times with dignity, not to be intimidated or frightened. What is necessary is to speak the truth.[1]

In speaking the truth, many dissidents from Central and Eastern Europe were lauded by intellectuals in the West. On the other hand, after the fall of communism in 1989, the writings of dissidents were increasingly regarded as historical documents of interest rather than political interventions of note. Dissidence was part of the ideological battleground of the Cold War and once the War was over all was deemed to be quiet on the Eastern

---

1. Patočka, Jan (1977), 'Testament', *Politique aujourd'hui*, 45.

Front. Vaclav Havel, Patočka's co-signatory of Charter 77, pointed out, however, that what Western Europe had failed to understand about dissidence in Eastern Europe would come back to haunt it. Havel's main contention was that the totalitarian regimes which had wreaked so much havoc in Central and Eastern Europe were the manifestation of the darker sides of modernity and that any attempt to think through modernity had to accept the unpalatable realities of coercion, terror and mass murder.[2]

Havel, in a sense, was aligning himself with a long tradition of Central and Eastern European writers and thinkers from Robert Musil and Elias Canetti to Czesław Miłosz and Jan Patočka who, alerted by historical experience to the nightmares of reason, sought out new forms of transcendence that would drive emancipation for human beings.[3] The drive for emancipation was articulated in a context of extreme crisis where peoples in the Soviet bloc were enslaved in the name of an ideology of emancipation. As Ireland goes through the most severe politico-economic crisis in its post-independence history, it is worth asking what kind of emancipation we might strive for and what the role of religion and critical thinking might be in a new project of human flourishing.

Political rationality

In July 2010 a detention order for a young girl in a County Cork industrial school was placed for auction on ebay. There was considerable adverse reaction from the victims of abuse in Ireland's industrial schools and comparisons were drawn with an earlier controversial auction of letters detailing the horrors of the Irish Famine. Davoc Rynne, the owner of the company, Irish Celt, which put the letter up for auction said in his defence, 'I can understand that [negative reaction] but we live in a capitalist society, so what can we do? I had to buy it.'[4] The MD of Irish Celt simply articulated what has become a fatalistic commonplace in

2. Havel, Václav (1989) *Essais politiques*, tr. Jacques Rupnik et al., Paris: Calmann-Lévy, p. 234.
3. Laignel-Lavastine, Alexandra (2005) *Esprits d'Europe: autour de Czesław Miłosz, Jan Patočka, István Bibó*, Paris: Gallimard, pp. 15-34.
4. McGarry, Patsy (2010) 'Industrial school order placed on eBay', *The Irish Times*, 17 August

late modernity. The writer and theorist Mark Fisher has dubbed this commonplace 'capitalist realism' which he defines as 'the widespread sense that not only is capitalism the only viable political and economic system, but also that it is now impossible even to imagine a coherent alternative to it' (his emphasis).[5]

To understand how even imagining alternatives has become impossible, it is necessary to begin by asking why one system has become both 'political and economic' in its expression? When neoliberal thought first emerged from universities and conservative think tanks, it was presented as primarily to do with economic arrangements. What neo-liberal economists sought was a radically free market, maximum competition, free trade, business friendly tax policies and a light touch regulatory environment. When neo-liberal thought became hegemonic in the economic arena, it began to shift from being a rationale for economic policy to becoming a fully-blown form of political rationality where all dimensions of human life were to be subject to market discipline.[6] Education, health, the prison system, social welfare, the security forces, all become subject to neo-liberal political rationality. As neo-liberal political rationality subsumes the State to its own ends, immigration policy is no longer a matter of humane response to human suffering but a cold calculation of the economic cost of keeping people together in the one place and the CEO of one company, Intel, commands more ministerial attention than all the faculty members in the Schools of Education in the Republic of Ireland put together. The native expression of this form of rationality might be termed McCarthyism after the type of instrumental cost-benefit analysis which underlay Colm McCarthy's 2009 report on the full range of the State's activities and the logic for the extensive cuts proposed in the report. The sole criterion for judging the success of a State under the new regime is its ability to sustain and foster the development and extension of the Market. Health, Education and Law Enforcement, which previously served different, autonomously defined ends (physical and mental

---

5. Fisher, Mark (2009) *Capitalist Realism: is there no alternative?*, Winchester: O Books, p. 2.
6. Brown, Wendy (2005) Edgework: *Critical Essays on Knowledge and Politics*, Princeton: Princeton University Press, pp. 38-40.

wellbeing, knowledge and wisdom, freedom and security) are now all subordinated to the one end, market sustainability.

One of the crueller paradoxes of the crisis which beset Ireland from 2008 onwards is that the crisis which directly resulted from the excesses of extreme neo-liberalism has led not to the de-legitimising of the rationality but on the contrary to an unprecedented intensification of the deployment of neo-liberal political rationality. As the Market proved itself to be the God that Failed, the response was not to dismantle a system or question a logic that had generated hitherto unseen levels of inequality, greed and environmental destructiveness but to use public monies to subsidise private losses and to introduce a series of austerity measures that primarily targeted public goods. In a sense, the Market has come to function as a dark version of transcendence, operating across geographical space and historical time and informing every aspect of the lives of human beings. Further confirmation of this phenomenon was provided in July 2010 where EU leaders met around the clock to discuss an aid package for Member States, the stated aim being to finish the discussions at all costs before the markets opened on the following Monday. The markets were treated as if they were a parody of a pagan deity, irascible, touchy, and only to be appeased with pledges, sacrifices and the burnt offerings of public services.

It is in this context that it is possible to argue that the greatest single threat to religious belief in Ireland is the relentless instrumentalisation of human beings implicit in neo-liberal political rationality. For when all is subordinated to the logic of the market, humans' only value lies in their market value, understood in exclusively monetary terms. The inhuman reductiveness of the Market also points up the falseness of the opposition in Ireland between religious believers and secular, progressive thinkers. A constant theme of public comment and mass media presentation is the pitching of secularisng 'pinko' liberals against 'hardline' believers of the nation's different faith traditions (more particularly, the dominant faith traditions). In this Punch and Judy Show of the Ancients and the Moderns, the enemy is alternatively the Godless or the Godfearing Other. The effect of this false dichotomy is to conceal the very considerable overlap in concerns and values between believers and progressive secularists, notably, the mortal danger posed to both by, what might be termed, Market Totalitarianism.

To contend that there is no alternative to the Market is to argue, in effect, that democracy is meaningless as democracy. If it is to mean anything, it implies a set of choices between alternatives. Free will, as understood by mainstream Christianity, becomes null and void as one is no longer free to will anything other than the Market. In a paradoxical way, the Market Totalitarianism which is the outcome of neo-liberal political rationality presents the ultimate triumph of the vulgar materialism which underpinned totalitarian regimes in the Communist bloc. All of human life and practices (superstructure) were reducible to the operations of the economic (base structure). The suppression of religious belief then was but one facet of this conviction in the supremacy of the material which is enjoying renewed vigour as an ideology in the fetishisation of the market. What I wish to argue for is the necessity of a new 'Culture of Dissent' in Ireland which will bring together critical believers and non-believers. In response to the Shock and Awe tactics of Market Stalinism I want to consider how a number of key concepts, central to both many forms of religious belief and to progressive politics, can enable a new coalition of the willing dedicated to the construction of a free, humane, meaningful and spiritually transformed polity and educational system.

Empathy
One of the most celebrated poems by the Polish poet, noted dissident and Noble laureate Czesław Miłosz (1911-2004) is entitled *Campo dei Fiori*:

> At times wind from the burning
> Would drift dark kites along
> And riders on the carousel
> Caught petals in midair.
> That same hot wind
> Blew open the skirts of the girls
> And the crowds were laughing
> On that beautiful Warsaw Sunday.[7]

7. Miłosz, Czesław (1988) 'Campo dei Fiori', *The Collected Poems: 1931-1987*, pp. 46-49, translated by Iribarne and Brooks, New York: The Ecco Press.

The title refers to the square in Rome where the philosopher Giordano Bruno was burned on charges of heresy. However, the square described in the poem is Krasinski Square in Warsaw, the site of a funfair in wartime Poland. Adjacent to the Square was the Jewish Ghetto and it was here on the 19 April 1943 that the Wehrmacht began to burn down the ghetto and kill its inhabitants. The poem juxtaposes the carefree joy of the city dwellers making the most of the amusements on a sunny Sunday afternoon with the unmentionable horrors ('dark kites') of the slaughter taking place only yards away on the other side of the ghetto wall. At one level, Miłosz's poem, written in the year of the destruction of the Ghetto, 1943, is a telling indictment of the almost casual anti-semitism that condemns thousands of Polish Jews to atrocious deaths. But at another, the poem is a more general snapshot of the terrifying consequences of indifference to the plight of one's neighbour. It is, above all else, a dark vision of the collapse of empathy.

A fundamental feature of a successful democratic society is the requirement for empathy. One of the duties of a citizen in a democracy is to learn what it is to be someone not like oneself and to be aware of the impact of choices that one makes on the lives of others. This can involve everything from the way we design entrances to our public buildings to the way we strive to avoid racial profiling in the policing of our streets. In a world of global interdependence, where our needs are catered for by people we will most probably never meet (the cotton shirt from India or the iPhone from China), forms of empathy need to be global as well as local. The capacity to imagine and understand the lives, feelings and historical experiences of others is crucial to the creation of sustainable human communities where citizens can remain equal in their difference. When we conceive of progress, it is typically in these terms. A particular group – the disabled, a sexual, ethnic or religious minority – is accorded rights of equal citizenship as a result of more inclusive forms of empathy. Conversely, bigotry, persecution, discrimination, exploitation are seen as undermining democratic promise because they fatally restrict empathy to privileged groups in a society. A singular contribution of the humanities and social sciences, from the disciplines of sociology, psychology, philosophy and

CHAPTER ONE   17

anthropology to the teaching of history and literature, is to develop and strengthen the empathetic imagination. Without such
imagination, the very cohesiveness of our societies is put in peril
and the ability for a country to function in a globalised world becomes highly problematic. The rise of gated communities in
urban centres all over the island of Ireland or the challenge, do-
mestically and internationally, of humane responses to migra-
tion show that there is no room for complacency.

What we witness under conditions of market totalitarianism,
however, is not simply the relentless celebration of individual
gain but the popularisation of deeply anti-empathetic forms of
Social Darwinism. What is striking about programmes from *Big
Brother* and *The Weakest Link* to *Dragons' Den* and *The Apprentice*
is that the supreme value is the survival of the fittest (the notion
of 'fitness' being variously defined). Rituals of expulsion, public
humiliation, vituperative forms of denunciation are standard
fare in the Circus slaughter of media innocents. Empathy for the
feelings of others becomes a positive obstacle to the onwards
and upwards strivings of individuals wholly devoted to a credo
of ruthless self-advancement. It is precisely this credo that is re-
pudiated by the teachings of the major faith traditions in
Ireland. What Christianity, for example, has tirelessly argued
for has been the absolute centrality of empathy – of doing unto
others what you would have done to you – to its message.[8] This
explains, in part, the immense hurt experienced by many believers on learning of the nature and extent of clerical abuse scan-
dals as they demonstrated, above all else, a catastrophic failure
of the faculty for empathy. The brutal, anti-empathetic thrust of
neo-liberal political rationality mediated by representations in
popular culture is thus deeply inimical to a core value of religious belief in Ireland.

The philosopher Martha Nussbaum in her recent work *Not
for Profit: Why Democracy Needs the Humanities* (2010) speaks of
the type of education presupposed by democratic self-gover-
nance. The type of citizen required is:

> an active, critical, reflective and empathetic member of a
> community of equals, capable of exchanging ideas on the

8. MacCulloch, Diarmaid (2010) *A History of Christianity*, London: Penguin, p. 88.

basis of respect and understanding with people from many different backgrounds.[9]

For a society to function as a democratic entity locally and to flourish as a community of equals globally, it must incorporate the empathetic imagination into every aspect of its educational practice. Empathy, in effect, is a value which offers a crucial commonality to believers and progressive non-believers alike as they collectively resist the destruction of their capacity to care for and cherish the lives of others.

Responsibility
Michael D. Higgins, the Labour Party politician and NUIG academic, has argued that in Ireland, 'an enormous price has been paid for anti-intellectualism, which has closed out political theory, the best scholarship and celebration of the imagination'.[10] Part of the price was the collapse of the Irish economy and the need for an IMF/EU bailout in 2010. What was readily apparent was the serious absence of critical thinking, more especially long-term, structural thinking, from the private and public sectors. The recourse to ill-conceived short-term solutions and active hostility to any serious questioning of an unconditional belief in the wisdom of markets led to the spectacular and costly failure of the banking sector and an unprecedented attack on the living standards of the least well-off members of the society. However, what the crisis revealed more generally was a paradox endemic in everything from systemic failures in the health service to governance problems in major financial institutions. On the one hand, for example, the credit crisis was blamed on particular individuals – named bankers or property developers – who were said to have abused the system. The system itself was not to blame only the proverbial bad apples. There was nothing inherently corrupt about present banking practices only isolated instances of corrupt bankers. On the other hand, when any attempt is made to go after individuals, the causes of abuse are said to be so systemic and so diffuse that no one individual

9. Nussbaum, Martha C. (2010) *Not for Profit: Why Democracy Needs the Humanities*, Princeton NJ, Princeton University Press, p. 141.
10. Dillon, Paul (2011) 'Interview: Michael D Higgins – Ireland's "Political" Intellectual', *Village*, December-January 2011, pp. 42-44.

can be held to blame. The bankers were only following orders, it is not they but the system which is to blame. This dual structure of disavowal runs as a common theme through the Blood Transfusion scandal, the catastrophic failure of foster care policies in the Health Service Executive (HSE) and the controversy surrounding the bank bailout. The ultimate result, of course, is consequences without causes. Nobody is to blame but everyone has to pay the cost.

This systematic evasion of moral responsibility has corrupted the language of public life. Public figures who have been shown to have done something that is patently wrong will only admit to an 'error of judgement' as if morality was a form of cost-benefit analysis and they had somehow got the figures wrong. When women die from contaminated blood products, children's lives are destroyed by criminally incompetent fosterage arrangements and ordinary citizens face real hardship as they bear the collective costs of private losses, the sense of injustice is compounded by the abject failure to hold anyone to account. This, in turn, leads to an understandable and widespread discrediting of authority, whether it be vested in banks, institutional churches or the legal and medical professions.

The crisis in authority can, of course, be addressed in two ways. One way is to render authority more authoritarian by making the State and its agents more coercive in their response to forms of criticism and dissent.[11] Another approach is through the development of what one might term a sense of structural responsibility, that is to say, a recognition of how personal, moral responsibility is determined though not nullified by structural constraints. The development of this sense of structural responsibility is dependent upon the introduction of critical, Socratic thinking at all levels in Irish education. Underlying such an approach to thinking are three assumptions. Firstly, people who fail to examine themselves deeply and critically are more likely to be easily influenced by others as was so apparent in the widespread consumerist materialism of Tiger Ireland.

11. Cronin, Michael (2009) 'Rebel Spirits? From Reaction to Regulation', pp. 109-122, in Ging, Debbie, Cronin, Michael and Kirby, Peadar, eds., *Transforming Ireland: Challenges, critiques, resources*, Manchester and New York: Manchester University Press.

Secondly, a lack of clarity about values, goals, aims or objectives resulting from deep thinking leads to the temptation to defer unquestioningly to authority figures, whether they be political bosses or senior bankers. Thirdly, when ideas are left unexamined, the temptation is to treat politics as a purely agonistic exercise, as all about Them and Us, where personalities are everything and policies count for naught. Crucially, when ideas are arrived at rather than simply given there is a much greater sense of ownership. It is easier to feel responsible for values that are freely and deliberately chosen than for those that are imposed or that are vaguely sensed to be part of a prevailing zeitgeist. The implication is that the sense of personal responsibility for deeds resulting from these values is all the greater in that there is a thoughtful engagement in the elaboration of the values themselves.

Central to the development of critical thinking must be an awareness of the structures that govern our lives. This is why I use the term 'structural' responsibility. If we are not aware of how larger politico-economic arrangements inform our lives then our notion of responsibility diminishes to a form of therapeutic individualism where the individual becomes the alpha and omega of the self-help industry. Nothing exists outside the mediated torments of the flattered self as exemplified by the relentless confessionalism on our airwaves. It is clear from the teachings of the dominant faith traditions in Ireland that believers are held to be accountable for their acts and that the teaching of religious morality is about, amongst other things, defining the nature and extent of a believer's responsibility with respect to thoughts and deeds. Faith traditions, however, not only counsel against narcissistic individualism. They also offer their own version of structural responsibility.

Diarmaid MacCulloch in his discussion of Greek influences on Judaism and Christianity argues that Plato's 'view of reality and authenticity propelled one basic impulse in Christianity, to look beyond the immediate and everyday to the universal and ultimate'.[12] Plato's view was articulated in his parable of the Cave where the particular phenomena humans observe are shadows of their ideal Forms which represent a truer and higher

---

12. MacCulloch, *A History of Christianity*, p. 31.

form of reality than the ones we habitually know. This would influence the development of the allegorical method of interpreting scripture amongst the sizeable Jewish diaspora in Greek-speaking Alexandria and the method would be later practised by converts to Christianity.[13] Thus, a fundamental tenet of scriptural practice in Christianity is to look beyond circumstance and contingency to larger structures of significance. The notion of responsibility only makes sense in terms of these larger structures of significance that are the articles of Christian faith and belief.

If believers and progressive non-believers alike are committed to a strong sense of responsibility, this must inevitably bring them into conflict with vested interests which as recent history has shown in Ireland are extremely reluctant to be held accountable or responsible for their actions. Implicit in a renewed commitment to responsibility is the recognition of the ontological necessity of conflict in society, a notion that might on first reading appear somewhat objectionable.

Conflict

A substantial section of bookshops in many richer countries is given over to self-help manuals. Implicit in these manuals is the notion that there is an ideal self which is somewhat out of kilter because it lacks confidence, vitamin B, the X factor or has failed to dejunk its life. 'I am not myself today' implies that there is a unitary, consensual self which is the desirable default value for the good life. That is to say, reading the right book, taking the right therapy, buying the right product, will lead to the finding of a 'true self' beyond disharmony or conflict. This psychologised consensualism finds its correlative at a political level in the notion that representative democracy consists of a collection of points of view which are all equally valid. The point of view of the workers' representative where 2,000 jobs have been delocalized is as valid as that of the corporate vice-president who has engineered the 'rationalization'. So everybody gets to have their say. But what they are saying is that real conflict is no longer acceptable. In other words, in reality, points of view are

---

13. MacCulloch, *A History of Christianity*, p. 69.

irreducible, as speakers are situated very differently, both materially and structurally. The false symmetrization of the mediasphere, however, conceals the very genuine conflict of interests through the irenic fiction of the representative soundbite. In another version of the tyranny of compliance, when social movements oppose government measures, such as penalising public sector workers for the financial irresponsibility of the private sector, government spokespersons and stockbroker economists talk about a 'communications deficit.' If only the people understood what they were doing, they would realise it was ultimately for their own good. Opposition can only be conceived of as cussedness or stupidity. No allowance is made for the fact that there are grounded material interests and structural conditions which make opposition not only inevitable but vital.

As even the most rudimentary exercise in the study of others soon reveals, understanding is above all an initiation into unsuspected complexity. The simplest of situations involving other humans turns out to be not as straightforward as we thought. What this schooling in complexity reveals is the radical insufficiency of cultural shorthand. That is to say, the cultural categorisation of society as made of recognisable types designated by labels, 'dyslexic', 'epileptic', 'Paddy', 'Gay', 'Muslim', reduces the multi-dimensional complexity of humans to one defining trait. Once a person is described using one of these labels, it is suggested that is all you need to know about them. They become transparent. Thus, if someone is 'Muslim' or 'Catholic', they must be by definition, bigoted, anti-modern, misogynist and obscurantist. What gay rights activists and the womens' movement, for example, in various parts of the globe and at different times have attempted to do is to restore multi-dimensionality and complexity to the lives of human beings who were deemed to be instantly intelligible as 'gay' or 'woman', gender or sexual orientation revealing all that was necessary to know about a person.

A multi-dimensional perspective on humans means opening up the infinite, internally conflicted, shifting desires, ideals and interests of complex, human beings in the lifeworld. It means resisting the quantitative policing of one-dimensional clinical labels ('autistic') or social typing ('deviant'), to restore the infinitely rich constellation of human experience and possibility. It is in this respect that the current vogue for 'transparency' is a form of blindness that is more to do with the coercive narratives of macro-modernity (name and shame) than with any desire to account for the exquisite detail of human fullness. Putting a figure on a number of articles published or on the amount of minutes spent in consultation may make the education or health service transparent to auditors but it makes them and the society that pays their inflated fees blind to the open-ended multi-dimensionality of genuine education and healthcare.

Implicit in the understanding of humans advanced here, is the inevitability, the necessity indeed, of conflict. As Angélique del Rey and Miguel Benasayag have pointed out, part of the work of mourning for humanity is the acknowledgement that there will never be perpetual peace. Each time, they note, that there is a 'war to end all wars' which aims at bringing about the reign of everlasting peace, the scale of destruction and human suffering is greater than ever before.[14] This observation is crucial as an attention to the local, the micro, 'small' places, 'small' nations can lead to a kind of consensual smugness in the present or a censorious nostalgia with respect to the past when no false note was to be heard and everyone lived happily before in the green houses on the prairie. Local community does not entail an end to dissent. Much of the disappointed reaction of post 1968 activists was partly to do with an overly benign notion of community. Having overly idealized the small community they could not tolerate the inevitable and indeed desirable persistence of difference and conflict. The notion that having found the larger group difficult it is possible to retreat to the haven of your 'own' – peer group, buddies, family – and expect the comforts of uncomplicated, consensual intimacy, is to invite the counter-movement of disappointment. However, it is important to move the notion of conflict beyond the binary logic of specular confrontation where entities with fixed identities face up to each other in a zero sum of binary opposition. Conflict from the viewpoint of richly differentiated human subjects is not confrontation, it is conflict as engagement with the multidimensionality of human beings, their texts, languages and cultures. It resists

14. Benasayag, Miguel and del Rey, Angélique (2007) *L'éloge du conflit*, Paris: La Découverte, p. 56.

the culturalist versions of contemporary biopower which in the name of avoiding a 'clash of civilisations' presents all conflict as confrontation through the binary stereotyping of Us and Them. The ultimate triumph of dictatorships as Miguel Benasayag and Angélique del Rey have pointed out is to present their opponents as pure adversaries.[15] Confrontation thus invariably leads to elimination.

An agonistic conception of human community which runs directly counter to the beatific visions of universal understanding underlying many public pronouncements on the topic of globalization, takes as a basic premise the incomprehensibility of the other. That is to say, human interaction is not simply the revelation of what is already there. The reason is that in the movement to engage with the complex being of others, in the creation of some form of shared sense, some degree of commonality, the operation is not one of uncovering a universal substrate, waiting to be revealed in its pre-formed state, but the contingent construction of bottom-up commonality.

The recent history of Northern Ireland has, understandably, given conflict a bad name in Ireland. Indeed, the whole period of suffering and violence has often been summed in that one word, the 'Conflict'. Churchmen from all sides worked to bring an end to the misery that resulted from inter-communal hatred. However, the natural ally of conflict is not hatred but dissent. Believers by acknowledging the infinite mystery of the divine made incarnate acknowledge the multi-dimensionality of humans mentioned earlier. Accepting the necessity of conflict is recognising the need for both believers and non-believers alike to protect the multi-dimensionality of the human and challenge the murderous shorthand of labels. As Stanley Milgram showed in his famous torture experiments and Solomon Asch demonstrated in his work on the reception of visual information, it often only takes one dissenting voice to prevent a group of people from erroneously misinterpreting as true clearly false information or more worryingly, participating in acts of extreme violence against other human beings.[16] The participation by believers

15. Benasayag and del Rey, L'éloge du conflit, p. 109.
16. Zimbardo, Philip (2007) The Lucifer Effect: How Good People Turn Evil, London: Rider.

and progressive non-believers in an active culture of dissent is vital in an era of market totalitarianism where bearing witness to core values of empathy and responsibility and the non-instru-mentalisation of human beings becomes more difficult by the day. It is striking in this respect that one notion which occurred repeatedly in the lexicon of dissident writers and thinkers in Central and Eastern Europe was one that is central to Catholic moral teaching, namely, conscience. Ivan Klima, Czesław Miłosz, Karel Kosik, Arthur Koestler, Zygmunt Baumann all stressed the importance of recourse to conscience as a way of unmasking the public lie and establishing one's personal duty or responsibility to bear witness against what is manifestly untrue and dehumanising.[17] What is arguably central to the development of an informed conscience is the instigation of a cul-ture of critical thinking in our educational system at all levels.

Fear
Fear is predictably a great enemy of thought. It is difficult to think or believe freely if we fear for our life or our health or our well being. Yet, fear is the predominant note of our age. Climate change, calamitous forest fires, catastrophic floods, extreme market volatility, pandemics (AIDS, SARS, swine flu), chronic youth unemployment, the list of contemporary terrors is end-less. Each evening on the news, we are provided with updates on the state of fear. Each age, in addition, has its particular genre of fear. In Ireland, the Religion of Fear (1920s-1960s) has given way to the Economics of Fear (1960s-present), the Fear of the Priest superseded by the Fear of the P45. One could argue that the changing genre of fear corresponds to a fundamental shift at another level which is the shift from the figure of discipline to the figure of control. The figure of discipline is typically that of the worker as captured in Charlie Chaplin's *Modern Times* or the prisoner as depicted in Oscar Wilde's *The Ballad of Reading Gaol*. The figure of control, on the other hand, is the debtor or the addict. Characteristic of Ireland during the boom period was the prevalence of the figure of control as evidenced by the histori-cally high levels of personal indebtedness and widespread

17. Laignel-Lavastine, Alexandra (2005) *Esprits d'Europe: autour de Czesław Miłosz, Jan Patočka, István Bibó*, Paris: Gallimard, p. 112.

instances of alcohol and drug abuse.[18] Indeed, the French philosopher Gilles Deleuze has argued that in contemporary control societies, debt is the final form of enclosure, the ultimate form of imprisonment. It was the similarity of States of Fear in the East and the West that led Czesław Miłosz to ask the question, 'Why should we love societies based on fear, whether it is the fear of misery or the fear of the political police?'[19]

In Ireland, particularly in the post-Famine period, the Church was often associated with a regime of fear and punishment that has been well documented on the printed page and on the screen. This, of course, is all the more paradoxical or poignant in that the founding message of Christianity was one of hope, of the banishment of and resistance to fear. However, progressive politics in Ireland has promoted its own states of fear notably through an overwhelming emphasis on negativity. The problem with perpetual opposition is that the most popular word is no. Like Ulster before, the mind becomes captive to a monosyllable. In a society where the punitive superego has variously taken the form of the coloniser, an unforgiving Church or the sententious stockbroker economist, the tendency is for critique to transform itself into the self-hatred of powerlessness. A more radical move is embrace a politics of hope which involves saying not no but yes. Yes to a better, fairer, more sustainable society. It is obvious that Irish society is at a decisive moment. The decisions taken now will affect not just the next few years but the fate of the island in this century and beyond. The core concepts underlying a new political solution are arguably self-reliance, social justice and freedom. A new way of ordering political and economic affairs means leaving behind a sterile politics of complaint and offering a vision that is both positive and transformative. In this context, it has to be honestly acknowledged that certain forms of political transformation, not only on the right (neo-liberalism) but on the left

---

18. Ging, Debbie, Cronin, Michael and Kirby, Peadar (2009), 'Transforming Ireland: Challenges', 1-17, in Ging, Debbie, Cronin, Michael and Kirby, Peadar, eds., *Transforming Ireland: Challenges, critiques, resources*, Manchester and New York: Manchester University Press.
19. Miłosz, Czesław (2004) *Abécédaire*, tr. Laurence Dyèvre, Paris: Fayard, p. 41.

(revolutionary communism) have manifestly failed. There is nothing progressive about a politics which is scripted in advance by the social and political movements of the past. A truly radical politics is just that, a politics which may borrow from the past but is not a hostage to it, and more importantly, is a politics which engages with the unpredictability of the present in unpredictable and challenging ways. So what education in a new Ireland needs is the coming together of both believers and progressive non-believers in a mutual commitment to a message of justice and transformation underpinned by the shared values of empathy, responsibility and hope. As we seek to achieve this it is important to remember the last words of the Czech philosopher, that we should not be 'intimidated or frightened' and most importantly that we do not intimidate or frighten each other as we have done for far too long.

CHAPTER TWO

Catholic Education and the Primary School in the Twenty-First Century

Dermot A. Lane

The way we understand the Catholic Education today will influence how we answer questions about the shape of the Catholic primary school in the twenty-first century. Let me begin, therefore, by offering three quotations which summarise succinctly what I see as the challenge facing Catholic education and therefore the primary school today. The first quotation is from Jacques Delors:

> In these times of intense change, nothing is more difficult than discovering what should change and what should remain constant. Only education can mediate between the tendency either to rely exclusively on what is new or on its opposite, a conservatism that tends to turn entirely towards the past. Education alone has the ability to pass on to students what humanity has learned about itself while at the same time providing the tools that allow everyone to face a future that is both new and uncertain.[1]

Note how Delors emphasises education as a process of passing on what humanity has learned about itself. It is a central conviction of Catholic education that humanity learned something decisive about itself in the story of Jesus of Nazareth, crucified and risen, and alive in the Spirit. Catholic primary schools, therefore, are committed to keeping the disturbing, liberating and healing memory of Jesus alive in our world. Memory is a key element in Catholic education. My second quotation comes from Mary Warnock:

> I have ... come very strongly to believe that it is the cultivation of imagination which should be the chief aim of

---

1. J. Verstraeten and Maria Duffy ed., *European Ethics Network Vademecum 2002-2003: Socrates/Erasmus Thematic Network,* (Leuven, 2002), p. 2.

education ... We have a duty to educate the imagination above all else ... So imagination ... is necessary ... if we are to see the world as significant of something unfamiliar, if we are ever to treat the objects of perception as symbolising ... things other than themselves.[2]

Part of the failure in Catholic education today, at different levels in the life of the Church, is due to a crisis of the imagination. In some instances, Catholic education has become stuck in a pre-modern social imaginary.[3] In particular, Catholic education is often locked up in a literal, non-symbolic world which no longer makes sense in the new, post-modern world in which we live in the twenty-first century. It is above all else the imagination, and not the intellect and not the cold, clinical rationality of the Enlightenment, that will enable us to move beyond the mundane secularity of modernity, to open up new levels of meaning, beauty and truth.

Putting together these two quotations we come up with a vision of Catholic Education, and in particular the Catholic primary school, as that which effects a creative unity between memory and imagination, between tradition and innovation, between the liberating narrative of Jesus Christ as the Wisdom of God and the creative insertion of that healing memory into the understanding of self, community and the cosmos.

It took the genius of Patrick Kavanagh to point out that 'On the stem of memory, creative imaginations flourish.'[4] Something similar is found in Augustine's *Confessions* where he emphasises the unity of memory and imagination in the coming to be of awareness and knowledge of the self and God. I want to suggest even at this stage in my paper that memory and imagination must be key elements within any reconstruction of Catholic primary school for the third millennium.

My third quotation is taken from the Second Vatican Council which says 'the Church always has the duty of scrutinising the

2. Mary Warnock, *Imagination*, (London: Faber and Faber, 1976), pp. 9-10.
3. On the difference between the pre-modern and modern social imaginary see Charles Taylor, *A Secular Age*, (London: The Belknap Press of Harvard University Press, 2007), pp. 159-211.
4. Patrick Kavanagh, Why Sorrow, *Patrick Kavanagh: The Complete Poems*, (Kildare: Newbridge, 1972/1984), p. 176.

signs of the times and of interpreting them in the light of the Gospel.'[5] It is only when the Church seeks to acknowledge and understand the complexity of the society in which it exists that it can become a significant player in education. It is not enough, in this era of exploding new knowledge and information, simply to repeat the past in the present; instead the vitality of Catholic education is found in its capacity to effect a transformation of the present through the prophetic, creative and redemptive elements of the Good News of Jesus Christ, who is always active in surprising ways through the Spirit in the Church and the world.

There have been significant developments in Irish education initiated by the State in the last decade or so. These include the publication of:

- *1999 Primary School Curriculum*
- *Education Welfare Act*, 2000
- *White Paper on Adult Education*, 2001
- *Education for People with Special Education Needs*, 2004
- *NCCA Intercultural Education in the Primary School*, 2005
- *National Childcare Strategy, 2006-2010,* Office of the Minister for Children, 2006

Alongside these documents there has been also the establishment of the National Association of Principals and Vice Principals of Secondary Schools (1998), the coming into being of Irish Primary Principals' Network (2000), the establishment of the National Framework of Qualifications (2004), the new Teaching Council (2005) which was launched on 28 March 2006, and the establishment of the Forum on Patronage and Pluralism (2011). These developments are to be welcomed and are changing for the better the landscape of Irish education

On the Church side the following sample of important documents have appeared:

- *General Directory for Catechesis*, Congregation for the Clergy, 1997
- *Guidelines for the Faith Formation and Development of Catholic Students*, Irish Bishops, 1999

---

5. Pastoral Constitution on the Church in the modern world, art. 4.

- *The Catholic school on the Threshold of the third Millennium*, 2002
- A working Paper entitled *Towards A Policy for RE in Post-Primary Schools* (2004)
- *Catholic Primary Schools: A Policy for Provision into the Future* (2007), Irish Bishops
- *Vision 08: A Vision for Catholic Schools in Ireland*, Irish Bishops, 2008
- *Share the Good News: National Directory for Catechesis*, Irish Bishops, 2010

In Europe, there has been a growing awareness of the importance of Religious Education in schools in terms of promoting respect among the religions, supporting social cohesion within the mushrooming of multicultural communities, and generating an appreciation of ethnic and cultural diversity. In particular the Council of Europe, one of the oldest institutions in Europe, has taken a new interest in the relation that exists between religion and education. Among its publications the following should be noted:

- *Religious Dimension of Intercultural Education* (Council of Europe, 2004)
- *Religious Diversity and Intercultural Education: A Reference book for schools*, J. Keast, ed., (Council of Europe, 2007)
- *The Toledo Guiding Principles on Teaching about Religions and Beliefs in Public Schools* (Office for Democratic Institutions and Human Rights, 2007)
- *Recommendation CM(2008)12 of the committee of ministers to member states on the dimension of religions and non-religious convictions within intercultural education*

I mention these developments simply to highlight the fact that while there has been progress in matters educational in Church and State, insufficient attention has been given to them in public debate about education. It is as if these developments run on parallel tracks, inhabiting different universes, without any serious engagement between what is happening in secular education and Catholic education.

It is against this background that I would like to address four issues in this paper: 1) To describe some recent developments in Catholic primary education; 2) To analyse some cultural changes affecting Catholic primary schools; 3) To offer some concrete proposals for the future; 4) To outline some characteristics of a primary Catholic school.

PART I: DEVELOPMENTS IN PRIMARY EDUCATION.

There is an ever-increasing awareness and appreciation of the importance of Primary School education as that which influences and determines the future of a young person's life. Those who work in Primary education have a unique opportunity to make a difference in the lives of their pupils and a lasting contribution to society. Consequently, this is a time for increasing local support of the good work performed by teachers in Catholic primary schools and not a time for reducing or withdrawing that support.

As we know the majority of Primary Schools in Ireland are Catholic. The Catholic Bishops have led the way in calling for the provision of other types of primary education and have offered to transfer the patronage of a number of primary schools to reflect more evenly the changing landscape of Irish society and affiliation to the Catholic Church. Other types of primary patronage include Educate Together, the new VEC Multi-Faith primary schools, An Foras Pátrúnachta, the Islamic Foundation, and Church of Ireland.

As a majority stake holder in primary education, the Catholic Church has encouraged other forms of educational provision to meet the needs of an ever increasing pluralist, multi-cultural, and secularist Ireland. At present collaboration takes place between the CPSMA, the Church of Ireland and the Islamic Foundation as agencies of faith-based schools and this is to be welcomed. Other, alternative networks of secular education should also be developed to facilitate the needs of the Irish Humanist Association, atheists, and parents of other secular convictions.

Primary education has become a flashpoint in public debate. An example of this can be found in what became known as the

Dunboyne dispute(2002) in Scoil Thulach na nÓg which created a lot of media attention at the time and gave rise to some misrepresentation about the nature of Catholic education and sacramental preparation. This in turn resulted in an INTO Survey of teachers and a Report with interesting results.[6] This INTO survey of Teachers found that the majority are happy to teach religion in Primary Schools. However, a growing number of teachers in Primary Schools are, understandably, concerned about the amount of time given over to sacramental preparation and the lack of pastoral support from Parishes for the preparation of children for First Penance, First Communion and Confirmation.

A second example of public debate about primary schools was sparked by an article in a national newspaper by the Director of the Irish Primary Principals' Network (2006). This article sought to open a debate about 'the relationship between organised religion and primary education ... the provision of a proper chaplaincy service ... (and) a new model of shared responsibility'. The front-page headline in the same newspaper came out as 'Heads want Communion lessons to be ditched'.

A more recent example of public debate was occasioned by the publication of *The Ferns Report* (2005), *The Ryan Report* (2009), *The Murphy Report* (2009), and *The Cloyne Report* (2011). These reports provoked calls by some commentators to wrest all control of primary schools from the Catholic Church.

Over the last number of years there has been a gradual decline of the involvement by parishes in the support of Primary Schools. Examples of this decline can be found in the absence of a priest on the Board of Management, a reduction in the Chaplaincy service from the local parish, and a diminishing visibility of parish involvement in the local school. This loosening of links between parish and the primary school has had a knock-on effect on sacramental preparation.

This decline, however, is symptomatic of a deeper challenge facing the Catholic Church in Ireland today, namely the changing character of the staffing, management, and self-understanding of parishes. As is well known, parishes today, in the light of the declining number of priests, are in need of reform, renewal

---

6. See *Teaching Religion in the Primary School: Issues and Challenges*, (INTO, 2003)

and reconstruction in terms of personnel, mission and vision – something that Archbishop Diarmuid Martin has sought to address in Dublin by mandating the establishment of Parish Pastoral Council in all parishes (2005) and even more recently his call for regrouping of parishes in the Dublin diocese into regional 'clusters' (2010).

There are urgent issues to be addressed for the renewal of parishes in relation to lay ministry, faith formation, adult religious education, and chaplaincy services. Suffice it to note at this stage that movement on one or other of these later areas would be of support to the work of teachers in Catholic primary schools. The introduction by Archbishop Martin of a three year pilot scheme providing professionally qualified Parish Pastoral Workers (2008), the publication of *Be Good News: National Directory for Catechesis* (2010) by the Irish Bishops, and the establishment of the *Catholic Schools Partnership* (2010) are significant new steps in the service of Catholic primary schools.

It is unreasonable to expect Catholic teachers to undertake responsibility for sacramental preparation of pupils in primary schools without support from the local parish. Further, this lack of support from parishes in some instances is compounded by the absence of support from parents. At present the three agencies of Catholic education namely the school, the parish and the home are in danger of continuing to exist as 'islands apart' (M. Kennedy). This is one of the urgent challenges facing Catholic primary education today.

PART II: CULTURAL CHANGES AFFECTING
CATHOLIC PRIMARY EDUCATION.

I now wish to outline some of the cultural changes taking place in Ireland that have a bearing on the Catholic primary school. It is necessary to understand the culture around us before it can be educated and evangelised. Several documents from the Catholic Church since Vatican II have pointed out that a faith that is not inculturated is not a living faith. So how do we read the cultural changes in modern and post-modern Ireland? Here are some pointers, just pointers!

1. From a sociological point of view it is extremely difficult to the describe accurately what is happening in Ireland at this time because of the pace of the changes occurring: economic development and expansion from 2000-2008 and since then the onset of a dramatic economic recession with far reaching consequences arising from a bailout of the domestic economy and the banking system by the EU, IMF and ECB. This economic crisis has exposed the lawlessness of unbridled capitalism and the heartlessness of market-forces. Since all institutions, political, economic, medical, banking and ecclesial, have been found wanting, the reinvention of Ireland has suddenly moved to the centre of the national stage. Whether Christian faith can play a part in this much needed reimagining of who we are as a people is a major challenge facing all of the Christian churches in Ireland.

It is my conviction that Christian faith and education have a vital contribution to make to the reconstruction of Irish identity at this defining moment in history. Christian faith has resources (ethical, prophetic and transcendent) that should be a part of the national dialogue seeking to reshape Irish life. These resources should be brought to bear in a necessary critique of market-driven-capitalism; in the promotion of the common good, social solidarity, and community cohesion. Christian faith has a vision that should be part of the conversation aiming to reinvent national life. This vision of Christian faith includes the Sermon on Mount, the Parable in the Gospel of Mathew about the social gathering and judgement of humanity at the end of time, the teaching of Jesus about the Reign of God as both immanent and transcendent, and the realisation of this vision in the death and Resurrection of Jesus. In making these claims we are not suggesting that Christian faith has a blue print for society or that it can offer a solution to current complex crises. It does, however, have a deep sense of what is not acceptable and of what offends against the equality and dignity of all, and it also has a passionate commitment in theory and practice to the primacy of justice within any reshaping of society.

To deprive children of this vision of fairness, to omit the story of Jesus and his proclamation of the Good News to the poor and the blind and deaf would be an impoverisation of memory and a curtailment of imagination. It should not be forgotten that it has always been in the interest of the 'powers and principalities' of this world to silence the prophetic and unsettling memory of Jesus as the Christ.

In the context of faith and Church it seems fairly accurate to say that the Irish situation is increasingly like that of Europe, in which, as one sociologist puts it, 'God is neither as dead nor as alive as some now maintain'. There is now a confusingly wide spectrum of religious sensibilities present in Ireland, which range from religious fundamentalism to secular relativism, accompanied by varying degrees of apathy and commitment. Within this spectrum one finds the phenomena of 'believing without belonging', the existence of a vague religiosity, a supermarket approach to belief, and a deep disaffection with organised religion. Some discern 'a crisis of transmission' in general within society, and in particular in the areas of numeracy and literacy, including religious literacy. Others point to a new interest in religion in contrast to the predicted disappearance of religion through secularisation.[7]

2. Ireland has become almost overnight a pluralist, multi-cultural, and secular society. This means that the Church must recognise that it no longer has a monopoly on education and can no longer assume to hold a privileged position. From now on, Catholic education must recognise itself as one player among many, a voice within a variety of voices, learning to welcome pluralism, value difference, and appreciate otherness. I believe that Catholic education can make a more distinctive contribution to Irish society from within this pluralist, multi-cultural and post-modern context. Catholic education within this radically new context will become more self-conscious of its own particular identity. Some may see this as a threat – I see it as a unique opportunity to rediscover the authentic specificity of Catholic identity. It may come as a surprise to some to learn that the Catholic Church is no stranger to dialogue with culture and other religions. In many places the Church has been a pioneer in promoting inter-religious dialogue internationally. Inter-faith-dialogue is a part of the teaching and practice of the Catholic Church since the Second Vatican Council (1962-1965).

7. See Lieven Boeve, Religion after Detraditionalization: Christian Faith in a Post-Secular Europe, *Irish Theological Quarterly*, vol. 70/2, 2005.

3. A third significant shift, indeed a paradigm shift, has taken place within education in the last ten years, and this is best summed up in terms of a move from imparting and handing down knowledge to a new focus on learning and teaching. Part of this shift includes the momentous move towards information technology as an instrument of learning, a recognition of the existence of multiple intelligences among all the pupils, and new appreciation of visual education as a stimulus of the imagination. Within educational circles, learning is now seen as a life-long continuum from the cradle to the grave. Adult education is no longer understood as an optional add-on to schooling but as something intrinsic to life itself. This new perception of the centrality of life-long-learning is already affecting the structure of school curricula through the work of the National Framework of Qualifications. This shift, of course, has very significant implications for the way we understand Catholic primary education in the future. In the past the RE syllabus of the primary school tried to cover too much with very little real learning. In the future, it is likely that less will be seen as more!

This shift also calls for a change in the philosophy of education operative in Catholic schools. In the future the role of the Catholic primary school will be as much to light a fire in the minds of young people, so that they will leave primary school with hungry spirits, restless hearts, inquisitive intellects, and creative imaginations, as it is to communicate the content of faith. In this way young people going into Second Level schools will know that there is more to education than just the information society, more to education than just an economy based knowledge, more to education than just the service of the economy.

4. Since Ireland became a wealthy nation through the so-called 'successes' of the Celtic Tiger economy, a new kind of poverty has emerged. Those who seem to have everything from a material point of view have often ended up having nothing from a spiritual point of view. Excessive materialism and greed are often an expression of a deep spiritual hunger in the midst of plenty. As a result of this new phenomenon, the search for new spiritualities is alive and well, while organised religion, and in particular institutionalised Christianity, is on the decline. Just

go into any bookstore and look at the books people are buying. The Catholic primary school in the future will need to bridge the gap that currently exists between spirituality and sacramentality, between the genuine hungers of the secular heart and the liberating gospel of Jesus Christ, between the restless spirit of so many and the practical wisdom that comes from knowing Christ crucified and risen. These educational and spiritual challenges have become even more intensified in the Ireland that has suddenly gone 'from boom to bust' in the short period between 2008 and 2011. The financial problems specific to Ireland in terms of 'the property bubble' and the banking crisis have exposed a deep moral vacuum at the core of several institutions and created a lack of trust in all institutions. A significant element within the Catholic primary school RE programme in the future will be moral formation.

5. There is the presence of a new subculture that exists outside primary schools which often runs counter to what teachers are trying to achieve within the school environment. This subculture is best described as one of experimentation, experimentation in relation to drugs, drink and sexuality. Within this subculture young people want to know how far they can go without falling over the edge, how far they can push the physical body without damaging it, how close they can come to danger without being devoured by it. This subculture outside the school is often fuelled by a morbid interest in the world of the occult, the existence of evil, and an extraordinary fascination with violence – all of which are readily available through videos, DVD's and the internet. This subculture is in some instances connected to a break-down of family life and, according to some, the absence of a male role model in the home.

6. A further characteristic of contemporary culture in Ireland affecting primary education is the presence of a hidden but deep crisis of faith among a growing number of adults. It must be pointed out in this context that because parents may have lost faith or given up on the Church, this does not necessarily mean they do not want their children to have faith and Christian values. One expression of this particular crisis can be found in the Irish poet, Dennis O'Driscoll, in a moving poem entitled *Missing*

God. The following is a sample of some of the striking verses in that poem:

> Miss Him during the civil wedding
> when, at the blossomy altar
> of the Registrar's desk,
> we wait in vain
> to be fed a line containing words like 'everlasting'
> and 'divine'
>
> Miss Him when the TV scientist
> explains the cosmos through equations
>
> Miss Him when a choked voice at
> the crematorium recites the poem
> about fearing no more the heat of the sun.
>
> Miss Him when we stumble on the breast lump
> for the first time and an involuntary prayer
> escapes our lips
>
> Miss Him when we listen to the prophecy
> of astronomers that the visible galaxies will recede
> as the universe expands ...[8]

A further expression of this crisis is captured rather graphically in an interview of Seamus Heaney in 2002 where he pointed out:

> I think the dwindling of faith and, secondly, the clerical scandals have bewildered things ... we are still running on an unconscious that is informed by religious values, but I think our youngsters' youngsters won't have that. I think the needles are wobbling.[9]

In my opinion it may be possible to steady the needles before they collapse if we can keep alive the liberating memory of Jesus Christ and activate the imagination of young people with the prophetic Spirit of Jesus.

---

8. Dennis O'Driscoll, 'Missing God', *Exemplary Damages*, (London: Anvil Poetry Press, 2002), pp. 29-31.
9. An interview in the *Irish Independent Weekend*, 16 November 2002, p. 9

A third expression of this crisis of faith can be found in some of the soul searching and questioning that went on in the media, particularly by Patsy McGarry and Vincent Browne, in relation to God and the Indonesian Tsunami in December 2004 and other 'natural' disasters around the globe such as hurricane 'Irene'. What is needed in this new cultural context from Catholic education is the introduction of people to a genuine experience of God, not as something exceptional, not as the privilege of a few, not as a phenomenon restricted only to 'holy' people, but a gentle, gracious presence that envelops all without exception and sustains the small planet we call 'Earth' within a vast cosmos of extraordinary order and beauty. In this way it might be possible to move beyond an interventionist image of God to a recognition of the Creator-Spirit as the One in whom we live and move and have our being as pure Gift. It is also important in this regard for teachers in primary schools to realise that they do not have to have all the answers to the burning questions of the day. In truth no one has all the answers and we should be wary of those who pretend to have them. Raising questions, walking in the dark with confidence, and struggling with faith are also a significant part of the Catholic experience.

PART III: A FEW CONCRETE PROPOSALS FOR THE FUTURE.

In the light of this overview of what is going on in education and in the light of this broad description of cultural changes in modern Ireland, I want to outline some concrete proposals for Catholic education and the primary school in the present and the future.

1. By far the most important and most urgent proposal is the need to introduce parish-based, ongoing programmes of Evangelisation and adult faith formation. The specific orientation of these programmes ought to be a matter for determination at local level to reflect local needs. What the Catholic Church needs to do most of all in Ireland at this time is to introduce people to a process of life-long Christian learning and life-long-faith development. What has happened in the last thirty years concerning school Catechesis and Religious Education now needs to happen in the area of adult Christian education in terms of resources, personnel and provision. This does not mean that the

Church should pull back from its present involvement with primary schools. There is a danger at present of going from one extreme to another i.e. of going from a strong emphasis on school-based Religious Education to a new emphasis on adult Religious Education, when in truth what is needed at this time is both school-based Religious Education and ongoing parish-based adult Catechesis.

The Church must learn to look in both directions, by continuing to support schools while at the same time addressing the educational and spiritual needs of adult Catholics in parishes. If this can be done, and I believe it can be done by recovering the memory of Jesus and energising the imagination with that memory, then the good work going on in Primary schools will bear even greater fruit in the future and adult communities of faith will become more vibrant and active. A good example of a parish based programme of Catechesis signalling what can be done has been made through the programmes of *Do this in Memory* and *You Shall be My Witnesses*.[10] Another significant start has been made through the publication of *Share the Good News: National Directory for Catechesis* (2010).

The huge challenge of life-long learning facing Catholic education in Ireland should be approached not in an ad hoc manner but in a planned way, not in terms of offering a few lectures here and there but according to the principles and methods specific to adult learning, not by someone who knows a little theology but by personnel qualified in the theory and practice of adult learning.

2. A second proposal concerns the importance of promoting Continuing Professional Development for all who are involved in primary Catholic schools. This would include Principals and Deputy Principals in leadership positions in Primary schools, teachers, Chaplains or Co-ordinators of chaplaincy services, and Boards of Management. At present there is insufficient educational support or spiritual nourishment of those in Catholic schools who are expected to lead in culturally difficult times and carry the burden in the heat of the day. In the past there were cultural supports and religious communities in the background supporting the leaders in Catholic schools. This has changed

---

10. Veritas Publications, 2004 and 2009 respectively.

and there is a need for ongoing structural support of professionals working in primary Catholic schools.

3. A third challenge for Catholic education is to enter into a new
relationship of transparent co-operation and partnership with
the State and its agencies of education. In this context it will be
necessary for the Church to represent both prophetic and institutional wings of Catholic identity, bringing together the Catholic
Bishops and CORI into a new strategic alliance and relationship.
An important step in this direction has been the establishment of
the *Catholic Schools Partnership* (2010). Equally important has
been the setting up of the Forum on Patronage and Pluralism in
primary schools chaired by Professor John Coolahan.

4. A fourth proposal is the need to correct some of the existing
caricatures and stereotypes of Catholic education operative in
the public domain. For example it needs to be said that Catholic
schooling is not about 'control', an emotive term, carrying negative connotations in a culture that rightly prizes freedom from
control. This so-called control of primary schools by the Church
misrepresents the practice on the ground in terms of the part
played by the Patron, the appointment of staff by open competition, and the role of the Board of Management. The Church's involvement in education is motivated by its commitment to a
particular vision of life and values inspired by the Good News
of Jesus Christ. To be sure the management of the majority of
primary schools by the Catholic Church is unsatisfactory for all
kinds of reason, especially in terms of limiting parental choice in
what is now a multicultural society. Cardinal Sean Brady,
Archbishop Diarmuid Martin and Bishop Leo O'Reilly have acknowledged this anomaly several times in public. Fr. Michael
Drumm, representing the *Catholic Schools Partnership*, has also
emphasised the need for greater choice for parents while cau-
tioning against a hasty dismantling of a system that by and large
has worked well. Drumm is also concerned that in bringing
about a change in Patronage, care should be taken to avoid
introducing a two-tiered system that could result in a situation
of social stratification within the primary educational system.[11]

11. See address of Michael Drumm, *Catholic Schools – Looking to the Future*, 8
May 2010 (www.ossory.ie/2010/06/catholic-schools-looking-to-the-future).

A second caricature is that Catholic schools are about a process of 'indoctrination'. This particular perception ignores the critical relationship that exists between reason and faith. To be sure when this relationship is denied then there is the real danger of indoctrination. The charge of indoctrination, however, fails to recognise that faith has the capacity to expand and enrich the horizons of reason and that reason helps to prevent faith from superstition and fundamentalism. Within this dynamic relation between reason and faith, the Catholic school seeks to open windows of wonder, to ignite a life-long search for values, and to introduce pupils to the Wisdom of God revealed in Christ. Further, the suggestion of indoctrination takes no account of the educational and theological integrity of RE as a subject in the primary school curriculum. RE follows the methodologies operative in other subjects and as such supports other programmes such as SPHE, RSE and intercultural guidelines of the NCCA and the DES.

A third stereotype is the suggestion that the Catholic school is a place of 'proselytism'. This accusation flies in the face of the teaching of the Church that the act of faith is always a free act and if it loses that freedom, or if coercion is brought to bear, then it is no longer faith but some form of ideology. The *Decree on Religious Freedom* from Vatican II clearly affirms 'the right of the individual to religious freedom' and that 'no one therefore is to be forced to embrace the Christian faith against his/her own will' and 'in matters religious every manner of coercion ... should be excluded'.[12]

A fourth caricature is the charge that Catholic schools are 'exclusive' to Catholics. This particular claim ignores the fact that Catholic schools in Ireland over the last fifteen years have been welcoming of pupils of other faiths and of none and other ethnic traditions. This welcoming spirit is a consistent theme in the literature about Catholic schools.[13] The truth is, in theory and practice, that Catholic schools are and always have been places of inclusivity, houses of hospitality to the outsider, and welcoming shelters to all who want to 'come and see'.

---

12. *Decree on Religious Freedom*, 1965, arts. 2 and 9 respectively.
13. See for example the *Decree on Christian Education* ,art. 9, from the Second Vatican Council (1965); *The Catholic School*, (1977), art. 85; *Lay Catholics in Schools: Witnesses to Faith*, (1982), art. 42; *Ecclesia in Africa*, (1995), art. 102.

A fifth caricature is the suggestion that Catholic schools are 'sectarian'. Concerning this point, it must be noted that ecumenism is not an optional extra within the Catholic school; it is rather a part of the teaching and practice of the Catholic Church since the second Vatican Council. Likewise, respect for and engagement with the elements of 'grace and truth' in other religions and a recognition of the action of the Holy Spirit that exists in other living faiths, especially the monotheistic religions of Judaism and Islam, is also an intrinsic part of Catholic education and schooling.

It should be noted that this dialogue with other religions is not about dumbing down differences. Rather, it is a process of discovering one's own Catholic identity though encounter with the other, seeking points of mutual understanding and enrichment wherever they exist, and acknowledging with honesty the presence of theological differences. To be Catholic in the future will of necessity require that one be inter-religious. It may come as a surprise for some to learn that the Catholic Church has been promoting inter-faith exchanges since the Second Vatican Council. Nobody has been more innovative and prophetic in this regard than the late John Paul II, bringing together the major religions of the world at Assisi in 1986 and again in 2002. Consider also his prophetic actions throughout the Jubilee Year: for example his visit to the Wailing Wall in Jerusalem and other symbolic gestures not only with Judaism but also vis-à-vis Islam. For many, his teaching and actions in the area of inter-religious dialogue are the central plank of his legacy and they have enormous implications for Catholic schools. This legacy of John Paul II has been embraced by Benedict XVI who, in Cologne in August 2005, declared that intercultural and inter-religious dialogue 'cannot be reduced to an optional extra. It is, in fact, a vital necessity on which in large measure, our future depends'. Catholic schools, therefore, should be leading the way in welcoming and respecting the pupils of other faiths in the newly emerging multicultural Ireland. There is a success story waiting to be told about the extraordinary way in which Catholic primary schools in Ireland have been able to accommodate so many of the new Irish from different cultures and religious identities.

These caricatures of Catholic education and schools do not help to advance an authentic dialogue about the merits or otherwise of faith-based schools. If anything, they show no awareness of what happened at the Second Vatican Council (1962-1965), or of current developments in theology and Religious Education, or of the social teaching of the Church on justice and ecology, or of the movements in ecumenism and inter-religious dialogue since the Council. Given these developments, it is perplexing to find the highly-respected Irish Human Rights Commission, both in its Consultative Paper in November 2010 and its Report in May 2011, using words like coercion, proselytism and indoctrination in reference to the teaching of Religion in schools. This offends all religions and Christian denominations. It is unfair to teachers to imply that they are involved in coercion, proselytism and indoctrination. What is even more bewildering is that during the welcome consultation that took place in November 2010 in Trinity College Dublin these caricatures were questioned by members of the Panel and by participants from the floor. One would have hoped that this valuable consultative process initiated by the Irish Human Rights Commission would have informed the 2011 Final Report. For some reason this did not happen. While there may have been some abuses in the past, these are now the exception. It is curious that the 2011 Report of the IHRC in its 'Recommendations' uses the word 'proselytism' four times and the word 'indoctrination' twice within the space of two pages.[14]

5. A fifth proposal arising from the above cultural changes concerns the new interest in spirituality. There is such a thing as a distinctive Christian spirituality which can only be hinted at here. Catholic schools need to introduce pupils to the rich tradition of mysticism that is a part of the heritage of Christian spirituality. We would do well to remember what Karl Rahner said over thirty years ago: the Christian of tomorrow will be nothing if he or she is not a mystic. When Rahner speaks of mystical experience, he does not mean some exceptional, unusual, or rare religious experience; instead what her has in mind is an experience of God available to all. At the same time, however, we must

14. *Irish Human Rights Commission Report*, May 2011, pp. 104-105

build on Rahner's advice by highlighting that the Christian of to-morrow must allow this mystical experience of God to inspire a new ethical, political and prophetic discourse in the public square.

A fundamental unity exists within the Bible and much of the Christian tradition on the close relationship that obtains between the mystical and the political, between the personal experience of God and prophetic action for justice within society, between personal spirituality and public witness. The Judeo-Christian tradition of spirituality refuses to allow faith to be side-lined by secular authorities or privatised by particular political agendas. It is in the interest of the market forces of the secular world to silence Christian faith and spirituality. At this strange and bewildering moment of history in Ireland, Christians through their faith and spirituality are called to be prophetic 'nuisances' in the public square.

6. One final proposal. The Catholic voice in Ireland is now one voice within a pluralism of educational voices. To engage with this reality of pluralism one must have a sense of one's own identity. Catholic schools, therefore, are not about being all things to all women and men to such an extent that they end up standing for nothing. Instead it must be recognized that it is only possible to engage fruitfully with pluralism from within a specific faith tradition. Dialogue within a pluralist situation is not about dumbing down differences to a bland blob; instead it demands a recognition that everyone brings something of value to the table and potentially comes away enriched through the encounter with difference. Those who suggest that the Catholic Church should get out of primary schools because of the new multi-cultural Ireland betray a curious innocence about what happened at the Second Vatican Council and the many developments since then in the areas of theology and inter-religious dialogue.[15] At the Council, the Church explicitly opened a new chapter in its own self-understanding, calling for a new dialogue between the Church and world, between Catholicism and other Churches, between Christianity and

15. A good account of these developments can be found in Patricia Kieran and Anne Hession, *Children, Catholicism and Religious Education*, Dublin: Veritas, 2005.

other religions, between people of faith and people of secular convictions, between belief and atheism. These new dialogues are an essential component of Catholic education and the Catholic school.

PART IV: SOME DISTINCTIVE CHARACTERISTICS OF A CATHOLIC PRIMARY SCHOOL

It would be impossible to draw up a complete list of what elements might shape the Primary Catholic School of the future. Local needs, established good practices, and the sociology of the local community would have to be taken into account in any outline of what a Catholic Primary School might look like. At the risk of being misunderstood, and of being quite incomplete, let me suggest, nonetheless, some distinctive and defining characteristics of the Catholic Primary School.

1. A Catholic school will promote the value of Religious Education within the school curriculum. It will prioritise the importance of giving pupils a holistic education: an education that integrates the value of the aesthetic, the spiritual, and the psychological well-being of pupils within faith-formation. The Catholic school will preserve the integrity of Religious Education as a subject in its own right within the school curriculum. It will also recognise the relationship that exists between Religion and Education within the school curriculum and see that this mirrors the larger debate about the relationship between Religion and Society.

Since the turn of the century, and especially in the light of 9/11, the Madrid bombings of 2004, the London bombings of 7/7/2005, there is a growing awareness of the dangers attached to isolating religion in society and the possible instrumentalisation of religion for political purposes that can result from such isolation. There is recognition that the marginalisation of religion and the privatisation of faith within society, so prominent in the latter half of the twentieth century, were not good for religion or society. Furthermore, there is a new appreciation of the positive role of religion in promoting social solidarity and community cohesion. This appreciation can be found among religious and non-religious political thinkers as diverse as Jürgen

Habermas, Charles Taylor and Terry Eagleton. This larger debate provides a new context for appreciating the importance of
Religious Education in the school curriculum.

The Council of Europe since the turn of the millennium has
been promoting a debate about the relationship between
Religion and Education, stressing the importance of the religious dimension of inter-cultural education, the educational
value of teaching about religion and from religions, and the role
of Religious Education in promoting tolerance, social responsibility, and community cohesion. This outlook on the relationship between Religion and Education was brought to the fore in
'Recommendations' coming from the Committee of Ministers of
the Council of Europe that were adopted in December 2008.[16]

A similar emphasis on the value of education about religion
and from religion can be found in the *Toledo Guiding Principles
on Teaching about Religion and Beliefs in Public Schools* adopted by
the Organisation for the Security and Co-operation in Europe in
2007.[17] Likewise, the findings of the REDCo Project (Religion in
Education. A Contribution to Dialogue or a Factor of Conflict in
Transforming Societies of European Countries), a three-year
EU-funded project (2006-2009), devoted to the study of religion
in schools in eight European countries, also recognises the importance of Religious Education in promoting harmony and tolerance.[18] Furthermore, the final Report and Recommendations
of the Cambridge Primary Review entitled *Children, their World,
their Education* concludes:

> On the question of Religious Education, we take the
> view that religion is so fundamental to this country's

---

16. Council of Europe, 2008. Recommendation CM/Rec (2008) 12 of the
Committee of Ministers to member states on the dimension of religious
and non-religious convictions within intercultural education (adopted
by the Committee of Ministers on 10 December 2008 at 1044th meeting
of the Ministers' Deputies).
17. Available online: www.osce.org/item/28314.
18. A summary of the Project and its findings can be found in Wolfram
Weisse, "Reflections on the REDCo Project", *British Journal of Religious
Education*, (March 2011), 111-125 and W, Wiesse, "REDCo: A European
Research Project on Religion in Education", *Religion and Education*, 37,
(2010), pp. 187-202.

history, culture and language, as well as the daily lives of many of its inhabitants, that it must remain within the curriculum.[19]

These developments, after a period of considerable disinterest in Religious Education, highlight the importance of taking the relationship between Religion and Education seriously within schooling. They all recognise that religion is too important to be left outside the classroom. To this new recognition of the value of education about religion and from religion, the Catholic school adds the importance of education into a particular faith-tradition. The Catholic school has always emphasised the central place of faith-formation as a moment intrinsic to Religious Education and complementary to the value of teaching about and from religions. Indeed, Catholic Religious Education, in the light of the teaching of Vatican II, and subsequent developments, requires respectful engagement with other religions.[20] Catholic education believes that education into the particularity of the Christian faith enriches the encounter with other religions and deepens one's respect for other faiths. It is doubtful that one can really appreciate other religions without some experience and understanding of a particular faith tradition.

2. A Catholic Primary School will be a place where people are aware of the rich tradition of Catholic social teaching: taking seriously the preferential option for the poor, according primacy to justice, and promoting respect for the environment. A Catholic school will be a community that is conscious of the requirements of solidarity: solidarity within the school, within society, with the earth, and with the developing world. A Catholic school, therefore, will have some contact with a Third World Agency such as Trocaire, Goal or Concern.

---

19. Robin Alexander, ed., *Children, their World, their Education: Final Report and Recommendations of the Cambridge Primary Review*, (London: Routledge, 2010), p. 268.
20. See Dermot A. Lane, 'Nostra Aetate and Religious Education', *Exploring Religious Education: Catholic Religious Education in an Intercultural Europe*, in Patricia Kieran and Anne Hession eds., (Dublin: Veritas, 2008), pp. 83-96.

3. A Catholic school will ensure that prayer is prominent in the life of the community, especially at certain times in the liturgical year. To that end, a Catholic School should have a prayer space/centre/oratory. This spiritual space will be shared with pupils of other religious traditions. The guiding principle vis-à-vis multi-religious-prayer will be the principle that guided the famous gathering of religions at Assisi in 1986: 'We do not come to pray together, we come together to pray'.

4. A Catholic school will be ecumenically alive and active in relation to other Christian churches. This ecumenical imperative arises out an awareness that the only way forward to Christian unity is through a deeper conversion to Christ for all of the churches, including the Catholic Church. So for example, the Week of Prayer for Christian Unity will be important in the life of a Catholic school. In a similar way, but on a different level, the Catholic primary school will be committed to encouraging respect for and dialogue with other religions, especially the great monotheistic religions of Judaism and Islam. Within this context the possibility of establishing 'friendship groups' with pupils of other religious traditions will also be encouraged. Respect for the festivals of other faiths will be promoted such as Hanukkah for Jews and Ramadan for Muslims.

5. A Catholic school will be, above all, a place where the memory of the Good News of Jesus Christ is at the centre of faith development and the religious education of pupils. In this context the fruits of the Spirit of Christ will be embodied imaginatively in the actions of the school community: love, joy, peace, patience, kindness, generosity, faithfulness, gentleness and self-control (Gal 5:22).

6. A Catholic school will give particular emphasis to the preparation of pupils for the celebration of rituals around the Sacraments of First Penance, First Holy Communion, and Confirmation. In doing this, the Catholic school has every good reason to expect support from the local parish in the preparation of pupils for the sacraments through such programmes as *Do This in Memory* and *You will be my Witnesses*.

7. A Catholic primary school will have visible links with the local Catholic parish in terms of receiving a chaplaincy service, in having representation on the Parish Pastoral Council or other parish committees, and through involvement on a voluntary basis with the Sunday Liturgy such as the Family Mass or the young persons' choir. The bond between school, home and parish will be promoted by the parish.

8. Above all else, the Catholic primary school will seek to ensure that every pupil will leave the school knowing, in theory and in practice, that, as Pope Benedict XVI has put it so elegantly in his encyclical, elaborating on the First Letter of St. John, that God is love – *Deus est Caritas* – and that this love of God has been revealed in Jesus and continues to be made present in the life of the Church through the action of the Spirit in the Sacraments, especially the Eucharist as the source and summit of faith.

By way of conclusion l wish to return to my opening remarks. There we saw that Catholic education invokes the liberating memory of the Christ-event in the celebration of Word and Sacrament in a way that activates the creativity of the imagination in the performance of justice for all, the care of the earth, and hospitality towards the stranger. Catholic education is committed to keeping alive the healing and prophetic memory of Jesus Christ as found in the wisdom teaching of his sayings and parables, in his inclusive table-fellowship with outsiders, and in his all-embracing proclamation of the Reign of God. On the other hand that historical memory of the Christ-event, active through the Spirit in the Church and world, must be inserted imaginatively into our understanding of self, society and God. The memory of Jesus, crucified and raised, will have a prophetic, paschal, and sacramental influence on the shape of the religious imagination in the twenty-first century. The various activities of the religious imagination will be synthetic, representational, and empowering in mediating the memory of Christ. Without this interplay between memory and imagination, between tradition and innovation, the disturbing but fascinating Good News of Jesus Christ will stagnate and appear as a museum piece of a bygone age.[21]

---

21. On the role of imagination see Dermot A. Lane, 'Imagination and Theology: The *Status Quaestionis*', *Louvain Studies*, 34 (2009-2010), pp. 119-145.

CHAPTER THREE

The Catholic Church's Current Thinking on Educational Provision

Bishop Donal Murray

Why Church Schools?
It is important to begin by reflecting about why the Catholic Church and other religious bodies should have an involvement in educational provision at all. That means reflecting on what we understand by education. Chief Rabbi Jonathan Sacks describes it in this way:

> Education is the transmission of a tradition. A civilisation is like an ancient but still magnificent building. Different ages have added new wings here, an altered façade there, rooms have been redecorated, old furniture restored ... We inherited the house from our parents and we want to leave it in good order to our children. We know that they will adapt it to their needs, indeed we want them to. Nor can we say in advance how they will do so or what the house will look like in the future. But as its temporary guardians, we know that we must teach our children its history.[1]

If this is the case, it is not surprising that religious communities should see education as part of their task. One of the characteristics of a community is that it has an educational function through which it leads its young members into an appreciation of the traditions and values of the community into which they have been born.

This is more than a question of a sporting organisation passing on its rules and its history and its cabinet of trophies. What marks off a community in the proper sense of the word from a group or an institution or a club is the quality of belonging which it implies. One does not belong to a community simply for a specific purpose – recreational, commercial or the pursuit

---

1. Sacks. J., *The Politics of Hope*, (London: Jonathan Cape, 1997), p. 184.

of some particular interest. One belongs as a whole person and relates to the other members as whole persons.

The State as such is not a community for instance. It is made up of many individuals and communities who work together as citizens to achieve certain political and social goals that are expressed in laws and economic plans and government policies. But being a citizen is not the whole of who we are. There are aspects of our lives into which the State has no right to intrude. One of the most important things in modern society where life has become so complex is to resist the idea of 'the Nanny State', the State that knows best about every aspect of our lives. There is more to us than should meet the State's eye.

The sense of community-belonging with the whole of oneself is found in a civilisation or a culture or a religious commitment. When Christians gather for worship, for instance, we gather with the recognition that we are mortal, that we are sinful, that our own resources cannot save us from evil and death, that our very existence is a gift of God the Creator and that our hope is in Christ who died so that we might live the life of the new creation. This is a statement about who we are, not just in one or other aspect or sphere; it is a statement of our whole identity, our very being.

That identity is not a straitjacket. The sense of being Catholic, or being Irish, for instance, is not an unchanging and unchangeable reality. Down the centuries it grows and develops. Through the events of history and through interaction with other cultures the house is redecorated and refurbished. Nevertheless, it remains the same house and for those who are Irish or Catholic it defines who we are. As the old joke makes clear, wherever we want to go, we have to start from here. Even if we wish to throw off our cultural or religious identity, it remains part of the story of our lives; we throw it off with a sense of going into exile – even if we do so with some sense of relief.

None of us came into existence as an isolated individual. We became aware of ourselves in an existing community, with an existing language, with traditions and values which we did not create. There are old legends about human beings who were not born into any human community – as in the stories about babies being 'raised' by wolves. Such people would have no language, no culture, nothing recognisable as education.

Education is a relationship between people, between teacher and pupil, among pupils and between all of them and the surrounding community. These are relationships founded on trust and on mutual respect for one another *as individual persons*, not just for our role as pupil or teacher. A great deal of education takes place through personal interaction which communicates values and convictions although neither party may be particularly aware of it at the time.

The point can be expressed in another way. If education is about the formation of the whole person, there can be no real education without a community in which it takes place. An education which would seek to start from a blank sheet would be an illusion. We begin our lives within a tradition which we do not create for ourselves. That tradition, our mother tongue, the experiences which have shaped us as small children, the capacities and potential we possess or have developed and the goals that attract us, none of these are created by us. We find them in ourselves and in our situation even though we can and do modify them, developing our capacities and skills, refining our motivation and our understanding of the environment and so on, but we cannot behave as though they are not part of the story of who we are.

We sometimes slip into an absurd idea of freedom, as if anything that has not originated from my own choice is a limitation on my right to be exactly as I choose. But that is not how human beings work. We exist within a tradition, with a native language, with a body that we did not create. And within our community we learn to speak and to act, we develop our skills; we learn what is important and what is peripheral. All of this is not a limitation or constraint – this is what makes it possible for us to communicate, to learn and to choose. We are never creative in the strict sense of making something out of nothing. We create by using our capacities, the raw material that is provided by our environment and the possibilities that we see. Then we may create something new, but never out of nothing!

How We Learn Who We Are

It is this context and history that has formed us into the people we now are. To begin as if we had no previous context that receives us, to which we belong, would be to diminish us by cutting us off from the tradition, the story, which makes us what we are: 'Deprive children of stories and you leave them unscripted, anxious stutterers in their actions as in their words.'[2]

Of course the most fundamental community, the most fundamental belonging, is found in the family. Robert Frost said: 'Home is the place where when you have to go there they have to take you in.'[3]

That is where we learn who we are; that is where we learn to communicate. Education is an activity which needs that sense of belonging with the whole of oneself. We easily say that education is about the whole person of the pupil. That means that it is concerned for the growth of the students in every aspect of themselves. It is not just about producing good citizens, or productive members of the workforce, or entrepreneurs, or people with particular skills. It is about educating whole people into the whole life of their community. Although that may be easy to say, it is a daunting yet a fundamental human task. That is why, of its nature, and most especially at primary level, education is essentially a family and a community activity.

The family is the first and almost irreplaceable educator:

> The role of the parents in education is of such importance that it is almost impossible to provide an adequate substitute. It is therefore the duty of parents to create a family atmosphere inspired by love and devotion to God and humanity which will promote an integrated, personal and social education of their children.[4]

The Irish Constitution, therefore, has it right when it speaks about primary school provision. It recognises that the State is not the primary educator. Its role is not to provide primary education but to provide *for* it, by supporting initiatives in society

---

2. MacIntyre, A., *After Virtue*, (London: Duckworth,1985), p. 216.
3. Frost, R., *The Death of the Hired Man*.
4. Vatican II, *Gravissimum Educationis*, p. 3.

and making provision itself only when that becomes necessary
and then only with respect for the role of the primary educators:

> The State shall *provide for* free primary education and
> shall endeavour to supplement and give reasonable aid to
> private and corporate educational initiative, and, when
> the public good requires it, provide other educational fa-
> cilities or institutions with due regard, however, for the
> rights of parents, especially in the matter of religious and
> moral formation.[5]

The main thrust of education does not come from the State
seeking to perpetuate the structures and the institutions and the
economy for which it is responsible. It comes from families and
communities wishing to keep alive the traditions and the values
and the knowledge that have made them who they are. The
Constitution recognises that this is especially important in the
area of religious and moral formation.[6]

In the Catholic Church, and indeed in all the Christian
churches, as well as in other faith traditions, the provision of education, in the widest sense and at whatever level, is central to
what it means to be a community of faith. Every Christian community is under the imperative to be missionary, to be educative, to make disciples of all the nations (Matt. 28:19).

This activity does not take place exclusively or even princi-
pally in schools. It is first of all an activity of the community as a
whole and of each member in his or her own way – parents, relatives, neighbours, parishes, dioceses, the wider Church. It is an
activity that marks every aspect of the community's life. That activity has been evident in the Church from the beginning:

> What was handed on by the apostles comprises every-
> thing that serves to make the People of God live their lives
> in holiness and increase their faith. In this way the Church
> in her doctrine, life and worship, perpetuates and trans-
> mits to every generation all that she herself is, all that she
> believes.[7]

5. *Bunreacht na hÉireann*, art. 42, 4, my italics.
6. Cf. also Universal Declaration of Human Rights (1948) 26.3 and UN
Convention on Economic, Social and Cultural Rights (1966), 13.3.
7. Vatican II, *Dei Verbum*, p. 8.

The Catholic School

Thus it is that the Catholic community, particularly at primary level, has sought to provide schools in which to further this responsibility of perpetuating and sharing all that we are and all that we believe. This is the context in which Catholic schooling has to be seen. The Catholic school cannot be understood in isolation from that context. It is an organic part of a community which seeks to share its beliefs and values with all its members, in a particular way with its younger members. Too often we try to think of the Catholic school and its ethos as if this were something that could be understood within the four walls of the school with no reference to the community of which the school is a part or the family which has entrusted the child to the school.

The most obvious element in the thinking of the Catholic Church on school provision is that, wherever it is possible, parents who wish it should have the opportunity to have their children educated in a school which lives in that tradition of faith. In saying that, it also has to be recognised that for all sorts of reasons, many Catholic children go to other kinds of schools. That raises a question that is not strictly part of our agenda here, namely how such schools can respond to the needs and rights of Catholic pupils.

In many different kinds of schools and in many parts of the world Catholic young people receive an education which is respectful of their beliefs and which gives them the opportunity to worship in the Catholic tradition and which builds up their faith. But there is a particular value in a school in which faith is integrated with the whole syllabus. The importance of that integration is not always seen and it is frequently misrepresented. We might begin by saying clearly what integration does not mean.

Sometimes people feel uneasy about integration of the curriculum because they fear that it may mean that every other subject must become a branch of Religious Education. Each subject in the curriculum has its own method, its own content and its own autonomy. An education that did not recognise this would be failing in its purpose.

Individual subjects must be taught according to their own particular methods. It would be wrong to consider subjects as mere adjuncts to faith or as a useful means of teaching apologetics. They enable pupil(s) to assimilate skills, knowledge, intellectual methods and moral and social attitudes, all of which help to develop (their) personality and lead (them) to take (their) place as active member(s) of the (human) community. (The) aim is not merely the attainment of knowledge but the acquisition of values and the discovery of truth.[8]

But that autonomy of the individual subjects cannot mean that they remain as isolated and unrelated pieces of knowledge. If education is about the development of the whole person then *in the pupil* – and indeed in the teacher – the subjects cannot remain simply as separate compartments. Each element of the curriculum contributes to the student's understanding of him/herself, of others, of the world, of the meaning of life, of God. If one does not recognise that, it is hard to see how one could regard these individual sections of the curriculum as contributing to the growth of the *whole* person.

The Vision

Catholic education begins with the conviction that the human person is not a series of unconnected compartments. Human life is not a chaotic pursuit of many unrelated and often incompatible goals. It begins with the recognition that our life has a purpose; we have a hope, which is large enough to respond to every question, every longing, every relationship, every suffering, every tragedy and even to death itself. Catholic education believes that:

This great hope can only be God, who encompasses the whole of reality and who can bestow upon us what we, by ourselves, cannot attain.[9]

The ideal situation for a Catholic child is that he or she should be educated in a school where this conviction is, so to

8. Congregation for Catholic Education, *The Catholic School*, p. 39.
9. Benedict XVI, *Spe Salvi*, p. 26, p. 27, p. 31.

speak, 'at home'. If what the child is learning at home about the love of God, about death not being the end, about right and wrong, is not being echoed in the school, if questions about these issues are not being dealt with in a way that is in harmony with the child's faith, this would be a recipe for confusion. It would also amount to teaching the child that there is a place – namely the school – where these beliefs are not relevant.

This is particularly important when that faith conviction is no longer 'at home' in the wider society as it once was. The expression of religious convictions is often accompanied by a somewhat embarrassed recognition that speaking like this may sound a little eccentric or old-fashioned or out of touch with 'the real world'.

The suggestion that religious belief is not relevant to large areas of life is the essence of secularism. It may sound like a recipe for tolerance and harmony – 'let religion keep to its place and we will avoid a lot of divisive issues'. The reality is that this amounts to a denial or at least a profound misrepresentation of God. A god who is irrelevant to some spheres or aspects of the creation is not God at all.

The Pastoral Letter of the Irish bishops, *Vision 08*, outlines the importance, in our context, of an atmosphere for education that understands the broadness and openness of the vision of faith and knows that it is not just a particular area of knowledge but the very meaning of our lives:

> In a climate of growing secularism, Catholic schools are distinguished by faith in the transcendent mystery of God as the source of all that exists and as the meaning of human existence. Thus faith is not just the subject matter of particular lessons but forms the foundation of all that we do and the horizon of all that takes place in the school. The Catholic tradition of which the schools are part has been continually enriched through centuries of reflection and development. This not only offers our pupils a rich heritage of wisdom but also gives them stability, a framework of meaning and a sense of direction for their lives in a time of rapid and often confusing cultural and social change.[10]

10. Irish Catholic Bishops' Conference, *Vision 08* (Dublin: Veritas, 2008).

Seeking the Truth in an Increasingly Plural Society

A Catholic school really living the Catholic vision is the ideal situation for a Catholic family, but the ideal is not always possible. We have to look at the reality of a society in which there are increasing numbers of people who do not share the Catholic faith, increasing numbers who are not Christians and indeed of people who do not have any faith. We also have to look at the fact that there are Catholic families for whom the religious education of their children is not very high on the list of priorities. We also have to recognise the various situations of Catholic parents, or parents only one of whom is a Catholic, in which the choice of a school 'that can best promote the Catholic education of their children' may present particular quandaries.[11]

All of this clearly poses problems not only for parents but for Catholic schools. 'Catholic schools are open to children of all denominations.'[12] That means that they are willing to face up to the challenges involved in responding to a situation of a plurality of faiths and of non-faith approaches among the people who may wish to have their children enrolled in a Catholic school. In particular, this can bring issues to be addressed both for the parents of children of other traditions and for the parish in which the Catholic school is placed. The Irish Bishops posed the problem as follows:

> It is sometimes the case that people choose the Catholic school simply because it is the only school available, and not because they wish their children to have a Catholic education. This can cause difficulties for parents who do not share the ethos of a Catholic school. It can also put an unfair financial and administrative burden on the parish. We feel that in such circumstances the Church should not be left with the task of providing for the educational needs of the whole community. As the Catholic Church accepts that there should be choice and diversity within a national education system, it believes that parents who desire schools under different patronage should, where possible, be facilitated in accessing them.[13]

11. *Code of Canon Law*, c. 793.
12. *Vision 08.*
13. Irish Catholic Bishops' Conference, *Primary Schools: A Policy for Provision into the Future*, (Dublin: Veritas, 2007), 5.1.

The difficulty in practice is to make arrangements that will be respectful of the primary rights and obligations of parents and families into the future. It is important to try to look clearly at some of the difficulties and misunderstandings that may arise as we seek to do so.

First of all we need to look at the most basic objection that is raised and which may even lurk in the minds of people who are firmly committed to bringing their children up in the Catholic faith: Is it necessary to bring religion, and the differences and separations that this implies, into the schooling of little children? Have we not seen in this country enough of these divisions and their tragic fruit?

The prevalence of that approach is not surprising. In some cases it may be a reaction to the Troubles, it is being expressed again in the light, or rather darkness, of the Ryan Report, but it also reflects an underlying presumption of the culture of many parts of the world, and most particularly of Western Europe. It is presumed that 'real' knowledge is that which derives from scientific proof and that everything else is opinion or even superstition. It is said, therefore, that if people want that other kind of knowledge taught to their children, they should do it in the privacy of their homes and not expect society at large to undertake a task that many of their fellow citizens regard as pointless if not harmful.

If we were to accept that as the basis for education, we would be relegating faith to an inferior level of knowledge. We would certainly have travelled a long way from a culture which believed that knowledge of God, however limited and inadequate, was the highest form of human knowledge.

> It may well happen that what is in itself the more certain may seem to us the less certain on account of the weakness of our intelligence, 'which is dazzled by the clearest objects of nature; as the owl is dazzled by the light of the sun' ...; yet the slenderest knowledge that may be obtained of the highest things is more desirable than the most certain knowledge obtained of lesser things ...[14]

---

14. Aquinas, *Summa Theologiae*, I q 1, a 5, ad 1.

What is at stake here is the human capacity to seek the truth, even to inquire about the ultimate mystery of existence. Granted that the pupils in Second Class will not be struggling with the higher reaches of metaphysics, but if they are not taught to deal with mystery and to wonder at things that cannot be proved or experimented upon by the scientific method, and if they are not helped to listen to the tradition of faith which sees God's presence and God's love everywhere in creation, they are not being educated as whole persons.

Over thirty years ago, the Bishops of the Netherlands wrote a letter about Catholic education in which they pointed out that the school should unapologetically make room 'for things that cannot be called directly useful or profitable ... A school hinders its pupils from discovering the meaning of life when the preparation for examinations is its only aim and a large number of passes its only pride.'[15]

The achievements of science should not be downplayed, but it should not be seen as the only form of knowledge, as the only valid way of seeking the truth. It is obvious that the kind of certainty that one can have in mathematics, for instance, is different from the kind of certainty one can have in the sciences, and is different from the kind of certainty one can have in ethics, and is different again from the kind of certainty one can have in speaking about God. This was something that Aristotle recognised nearly two and a half millennia ago:

> It is the mark of an educated man to look for precision in each class of things just so far as the nature of the subject admits; it is evidently equally foolish to accept probable reasoning from a mathematician and to demand scientific proofs from a rhetorician.[16]

When one does experience mystery and wonder, this opens up questions which cannot be fully addressed by mathematics or by scientific proofs. They are addressed at their deepest level by philosophy and especially by religion. 'Granny has died. Where is she now?' 'Who made the world and the stars and the plants and the animals – and who made me?' 'Why do people

---

15. *Letter of the Netherlands Bishops on Catholic Education*, 1977.
16. Aristotle, *Nicomachean Ethics*, 1.3.

get sick?' Or perhaps we may come across the child who asked the most basic question, 'Mummy, *why* is a cow?'[17]

To approach the mysteries of life and death and creation, to approach art and music and history and literature without any reference to the faith and the questioning of the people who speak to us in these cultural expressions is not educating the whole person of the pupil. A great deal of art and literature grapples with the unlimited longings of the human heart in tension with the all too limited realisation of those longings in our lives. To attempt to deal with these matters without ever listening to the echo of the pupil's faith and the pupil's search for the truth of God in them would be a failure to seek the whole truth about the whole person.

To put it another way, if we confine ourselves to a kind of knowledge which is scientifically demonstrable; if we regard the scientific method as the only way of arriving at real truth, then we diminish ourselves and devalue the truth about the human person.

It is man himself who ends up being reduced, for the specifically human questions about our origin and destiny, the questions raised by religion and ethics, then have no place within the purview of collective reason as defined by 'science' and must thus be relegated to the realm of the subjective.[18]

Those who do not Share the Ethos
The statement made by the Irish bishops in 2007 recognised that when, in the absence of a local alternative, parents have no choice but to send their children to a Catholic school, this can cause difficulties for them and indeed for the school. The difficulty is twofold. One aspect concerns the right of pupils to be withdrawn from classes of Religious Instruction or Catechesis. This right is recognised in the Constitution in the context of the provision of State aid to schools:

Legislation providing State aid for schools shall not discriminate between schools under the management of

17. P. Brown, quoted by Radcliffe, T., *Why Go to Church?* (London: Continuum, 2008), p. 49.
18. Benedict XVI, *Address at the University of Regensburg*, 12 September 2006.

different religious denominations, nor be such as to affect prejudicially the right of any child to attend a school receiving public money without attending religious instruction at that school.[19]

The increasing number of pupils whose parents do not wish them to receive religious instruction that is designed for Catholic children can make the logistics of this difficult, but since the right is recognised in the Constitution, one would hope that the Government might make possible the conditions to enable it to be recognised in practice. This might require additional space, additional supervision, or the employment of part-time teachers to provide instruction in the faith or values system of the families concerned.

In one sense this question of withdrawal from formal religious formation is the easier dimension of the problem. If the family find the Catholic *ethos* of the school unacceptable, however, there does not seem to be any obvious solution. If it is the expression of Catholic faith within the life of the school that is unacceptable to them, and if withdrawal from religious instruction is not enough, then it seems that one would have to acknowledge that this kind of school is simply not suitable for that family.

As I already said, an education which would exclude any reference to faith might sound like a reasonable solution which would allow all pupils to be on an equal footing. But that would be an illusion. There are many parents, not only Catholics – one thinks of Muslim families for instance – who would find an education that took place 'as though God did not exist' utterly repugnant.

Those who take their own faith seriously are better placed to understand the seriousness with which others take their relationship with God. I suspect that many parents of other faiths would be happier to see their children in a school where religion was taken seriously than a school in which religion did not figure at all.

An education that does not address the pupil's quest for the truth about the meaning of life is not neutral. The widespread

---

19. *Bunreacht na hÉireann*, 44.2.4O.

acceptance of the assumption that it is neutral is an extraordinary coup by those who argue for that position. Somebody once said that secularism has propagated itself by the utterly brilliant communications technique of simply assuming its case to be entirely self-evident! But it is not self-evident at all. Such an approach is one perspective among many on the underlying question of the meaning of human life and the meaning of education. It is an approach which says that fundamental questions can be adequately explored while ruling out any reference to God.

Education cannot be neutral about the meaning of human life or the about how it understands the human person. Does life have a purpose beyond our present existence and a meaning beyond what can be scientifically demonstrated? An education that would purport to be neutral about such issues would actually be stating unambiguously that these matters do not have the importance and the universal relevance which believers see in them. For a believer, the exclusion of religion, or the study of faith only as an objective phenomenon, does not meet the needs of an integral education. The question of our relationship with God is not an abstract enquiry. It is the most fundamental question about ourselves. The abstract recognition that religious beliefs are to be respected but need not be engaged with is in fact disrespectful:

> The abstract language of rights fails to enter into the depth of what Hinduism means to a Hindu or Confucianism to its devotees. It suggests that the particularities of a culture are mere accretions to our essential and indivisible humanity, instead of being the very substance of how most people learn what it is to be human. In particular it understates the difficulty and necessity of making space for strangers ...[20]

Like every educational endeavour, a secularist education would be based on a very particular attitude to the meaning of life:

> Either implicit or explicit reference to a determined attitude to life (*Weltanschauung*) is unavoidable in education because it comes into every decision that is made.[21]

---

20. Sacks, J., *The Dignity of Difference,* (London: Continuum, 2002), p. 62.
21. Congregation for Catholic Education, *The Catholic School* (1977), p. 29.

This means that the idea that there could be schools whose ethos would be entirely in harmony with the views of every family and every pupil is false. There will always be issues of an ethical, cultural and religious nature where there will be differences among the pupils and their families. The school can and should respect these convictions and perspectives, but this respect for convictions is not achieved by making them invisible and inaudible. Nor is it achieved by silencing the ethos of the Catholic school. On the contrary, the good school will positively seek to draw enrichment and mutual understanding from diversity:

> Catholic education values tolerance and inclusiveness in an increasingly multicultural society; it is open to generous dialogue with Christians of other traditions and those of other faiths and none, while remaining true to its own distinctive ethos... The schools see such diversity as offering opportunities for deeper understanding among people holding diverse convictions. They also promote the common good of society as a whole.[22]

There is a tempting short cut to that kind of enrichment – to try to teach every pupil about every religion with no commitment to any of them. People say that it is wrong to separate pupils and to 'create divisions'. It is sometimes claimed that this would be the path to harmony in society. But this would not be fair to the pupils, whether Catholic or others.

Divisions are not avoided by keeping differences out of sight or refusing to address them. Divisions can become sources of enrichment only if they are expressed and there is a serious effort to understand different points of view. But abstract description cannot capture the real significance of what faith means to individuals and communities.

Hatred and bigotry are the products of ignorance, ignorance first of all of one's *own* position. The person who, deep down, doesn't know where he or she stands is the one who will dismiss other people's convictions out of hand:

> In real life the people who are most bigoted are those who have no convictions at all ... Bigotry is the resistance

22. *Vision 08.*

offered to definite ideas by the vague bulk of people whose ideas are indefinite to excess.[23]

To leave the pupils with a mixture of different traditions without the possibility of standing in their own tradition and having a tradition to share, would be to leave them with an inadequate basis on which to relate. In order for people to engage constructively with those of different denominations, faiths and cultures they need not just a willingness to dialogue but also some grasp of their own tradition which they are bringing to the table. Without a solid ground to stand on they will either find themselves agreeing with the last thing that was said – even if it is completely incompatible with the second last – or they will become so insecure about their own position that they will be unable really to hear what the others are saying. It would be very unfair to young children to throw them into the arena of world religions without a sense of their own religious identity.

In speaking like this I am not pretending that there are no challenges in approaching things in this way. Nor am I claiming that Catholic schools always succeed in doing so. What I am describing here is the way things should be. To reflect on this is also to challenge ourselves as schools and as communities about the quality of our welcome for those whose culture or religion is different from our own.

Our reflection also reveals, however, that people of faith cannot but have difficulties with a system of education which does not see the openness of the human person to the Transcendent as essential to the nature of education. This means that the study of religion simply as a historical or cultural phenomenon is not educative in the fullest sense of that word. In other words it does not address the growth of the person of the pupil in his or her most fundamental dimension. A study of religious faith without commitment, without worship, leaves the matter exterior to the pupil as an object to be studied rather than as a personal relationship to be developed.

This is a crucial question when it comes to providing religious education for Catholic pupils, and for other pupils, in

---

23. Chesterton, G. K., *Heretics in Collected Works 1*, (San Francisco: Ignatius Press, 1986), pp. 201-202.

whatever new forms of schools will be established in the coming years. It will be very important to ensure that in any schools set up by State agencies, the Constitutional guarantee should be fully honoured, so that there is due regard 'for the rights of parents, *especially in the matter of religious and moral formation*'[24].

Bilingualism

The most fundamental danger about an approach which would exclude religious faith, at least in any sense in which it addresses the personal searching of the pupil and the deep mystery of his or her life, is that it empties out what is fundamental. This approach seeks to produce harmony and the peaceful life of society by removing these sources of division.

The problem is that what is being left out of the picture is the deepest motivation that human beings have – namely their vision of what their lives are about. A curriculum made up of separate subjects which are never seen in terms of the overall meaning of life, the overall quest for the truth, is the mirror of a society that lacks an overall vision. That lack can be full of danger, especially in uncertain times such as ours:

> It is when we lose a sense of vision that we find ourselves, in effect, without a map or a destination. That is when people turn to populist leaders capable of manipulating public fear, or to regressive identities and fundamentalisms that allow them to cope with fear by blaming some group or other for being the cause of the world's ills. These are possibilities that I never thought I would have to warn against in my lifetime, so great were the catastrophes they brought about in the twentieth century. But when feelings run high, memories are short.[25]

We can hardly doubt that feelings are running much higher and the world has become much more at risk in the short time since those words were first published.

There seems to be an insoluble dilemma in a society with a combination of competing visions together with a significant number of people who do not see the need for an overall vision

---

24. *Bunreacht na hÉireann*, art 42, 4, my italics.
25. *The Dignity of Difference*, p. 84.

at all. This leads to the strange phenomenon of the constant calls for strong leadership together with a deep resentment of any prospective leader who would dare to say that we should all commit ourselves to any particular vision.

Chief Rabbi Jonathan Sacks suggests a way out of this dilemma. In a pluralist society, he suggests, we all need to become bilingual. We need a common language of citizenship in which we can engage with people of other religious and cultural communities. But if we have only this language of the whole group of citizens, 'we have no resources for understanding why none of our several aspirations can be met in full and why we must restrain ourselves to leave space for other groups'.[26] Besides, it will be a language with no literature, no history, no culture – a language in which no community has lived the life of whole persons.

We also need another language, the language of our families and communities, 'where we learn who we are; where we develop sentiments of belonging and obligation; where our lives acquire substantive depth'.[27] All that I have been saying has been pointing to the need for this language, this mother tongue, to have a place in the language of education, and indeed to be as far as possible the language of primary education.

This is not in any way to divert education from the goals that society and the State rightly expect of the school. Of course education should seek to produce good citizens, people who are capable of undertaking useful roles in the economy, politics, media, and so on. What I have been saying is that if one were to make these the principal goals of education one would distort and diminish the meaning of education. The truth is that a healthy society, a harmonious society and even a productive society, is founded on healthy convictions and a healthy understanding of the truth about the human person:

> Authentic democracy is possible only in a State ruled by law, and on the basis of a correct conception of the human person ... Nowadays there is a tendency to claim that agnosticism and sceptical relativism are the philosophy and the basic attitude which correspond to democratic forms

26. Sacks, J., *The Persistence of Faith*, (London: Weidenfeld and Nicolson, 1991), p. 67.
27. *The Persistence of Faith*, p. 66.

of political life. Those who are convinced that they know
the truth and firmly adhere to it are considered unreliable
from a democratic point of view, since they do not accept
that truth is determined by the majority, or that it is subject to variation according to different political trends ...
As history demonstrates, a democracy without values easily turns into open or thinly disguised totalitarianism.[28]

To attempt to build a civil society on the basis that such fundamental beliefs and values are private matters and that they
have no place in education would be to build without foundations. These values are where our moral energy comes from,
from our belief as to what life is ultimately about. One wonders
to what extent the events of recent years in many parts of the
world, and not least here in Ireland, reflect the detachment of
these beliefs and values from areas such as economics and finance and ethical standards. We need to find a language in
which we can express our values and beliefs in dialogue with
those who do not share our faith.

The role of faith, the role of the Church, in all of this is crucial.
The Church,

> is called to contribute to the purification of reason and to
> the reawakening of those moral forces without which just
> structures are neither established nor prove effective in
> the long run.[29]

The Future Shape of Provision

To return to the question of school provision, it is very clear that
new forms of schools at primary level will be necessary in
Ireland. That is most obvious in new areas where the Catholic
Church cannot be expected to continue to be the only provider.

> In new centres of population it is incumbent upon the
> State to plan for the provision of school sites and to en-
> sure, in consultation with the various patron bodies, that
> there is a plurality of school provision reflecting the wish-
> es of the parents in the area.[30]

28. John Paul II, *Centesimus Annus*, 46.
29. Benedict XVI, *Deus Caritas Est*, 29.
30. *Vision 08.*

It is also clear that in some older areas there are families who wish to send their children to a school under a different form of patronage, which is not currently available to them. The interests of the Church in this situation are:

- that those parents who want a Catholic education for their children should, as far as is possible, have that option available in their area.
- that other parents also should have the choice of the kind of school they wish to have for their children.

Looking to the future it is clear that as Irish society becomes more diverse Catholic schools will not continue to be such a massive proportion of the primary schools in the country. The manner in which a greater variety of provision might be achieved will vary from place to place and will have to be discussed among all the relevant parties in each particular case.

It may be, particularly in urban areas, that, because of population shifts, demographic changes or changing parental wishes, not all the Catholic schools in the area may continue to be viable as Catholic schools. Clearly, this is a situation which requires a great deal of consultation with all the parties involved. Anyone who has been involved in the amalgamation of schools, or in making changes in the catchment areas or enrolment policies, for instance, will appreciate the delicacy of making changes. For instance, some of those who became part of the school community when it was a Catholic school and perhaps because it was a Catholic school, may have strong objections to its becoming a different kind of school.

There might also be a fear that the current ethnic or religious make-up of the pupils or the youth population of the area could change as dramatically in the next ten or fifteen years as it did in the last and that substantial changes may be made which later seem to have been overhasty. All of this will require careful assessment of numbers, projections and resources as well as of the nature of any alternative provision and of the real needs of the area:

However, such evaluation should take into account not only financial and numerical criteria but also a concern for those who are needy or disadvantaged. In certain circumstances it may be considered desirable to enter into new patronage arrangements, provided these arrangements respect the rights of Catholic parents, in particular in relation to the religious instruction of their children within the school curriculum.[31]

In practice this may mean the provision of transport in order to enable parents, whether Catholic or of other denominations or faiths, or of no religious belief, to send their children to schools of their choice. Where the numbers seeking a particular kind of school are too small or the distances too great it may not be reasonable to provide schools for every group of parents, but every effort should be made to facilitate parental choice.

It is important, however, that in an effort to please everybody, we do not succumb to the false assumption that a school in which there is no religious formation is somehow fair to everyone. Such a school would be fair only to those who believe that religious formation has no part to play in the education of children.

The interest of the State is in the formation of good citizens, but that cannot be done without setting out to form the whole person. The modern democratic State is built on foundations that it did not and cannot lay. It is bound to respect rights that it did not create and cannot abolish: the right to life, the right to respect for one's dignity, the right to equality before the law and so on. Pope John Paul II makes what seems at first sight a surprising statement:

> In a certain sense, the source and synthesis of these rights is religious freedom, understood as the right to live in the truth of one's faith and in conformity with one's transcendent dignity as a person.[32]

In other words, all of these rights grow out of the transcendent dignity of the person. That is the foundation on which the State, and all human society, is built. That is also the foundation of Catholic education.

---

31. *Primary Schools: A Policy for Provision into the Future*, 5.2.
32. *Centesimus Annus*, 47.

CHAPTER FOUR

The Catholic Church and Primary Education in Ireland: An Historical Perspective

Tony Lyons

Prior to the introduction of a state-aided primary education system in 1831, there had been a long tradition of state intervention in Irish education. The provision for primary education began in the sixteenth century. In 1537 Henry VIII introduced education legislation for the establishment of parish schools in every diocese in Ireland. This Tudor legislation provided that the schoolmaster should be an Englishman, or have English antecedents within the realm of Ireland.[1] These schools were first and foremost anglicizing and proselytising. They were essentially established to shore up wavering loyalty within the ranks of the Old English in Ireland. Ultimately, these schools failed both from the qualitative and quantitative points of view. Few were ever established and those that were often became tainted with corruption. These schools were funded by the Crown, but in significant cases the monies allocated to them were directed elsewhere by the local Protestant bishop who had responsibility for these institutions in the first place.

A similar fate befell the diocesan schools established by Elizabethan legislation in 1570. They too failed to live up to expectations. Neither these secondary schools nor the parish primary schools ever garnered any support from Catholic Ireland.

Later attempts by the state to galvanize into place a coherent network of schools had limited success. The Royal Schools of James I were established in the early seventeenth century, but they had a very unsteady foundation, never catering for more than two hundred students. In 1733, the Incorporated Society in Dublin for Promoting English Protestant Schools in Ireland was given a charter. These charter schools were for the education of

1. Donald H. Akenson, *The Irish Education Experiment: The National System of Education in the Nineteenth Century* (London: Routledge and Kegan Paul, 1970), p. 26.

the poor, and were free of charge. These were avowedly proselytising and Anglicizing. They were relatively successful and
some Catholics attended them. However, it is interesting to note
that none of these schools could have provided adequately for
the majority Catholic population. These were public institutions
supported to varying degrees by government policy.

The government's motivation in establishing or aiding these
institutions appears far from impartial, especially in so far as the
measures were aimed at undercutting the Roman Catholic
faith.[2] Nevertheless, we should not allow the impercipient nature of the government's motives to obscure the fact that the
state did intervene in Irish educational affairs at a much earlier
time than in Great Britain. Long before the nineteenth century,
the provision of public educational institutions was an accepted
weapon in the Irish state's arsenal of social control devices.[3]
Failure to recognise this would make it impossible to understand why the state intervened in the provision of elementary
education under the National School system of the 1830s.

The Eighteenth Century and the Hedge Schools
In Irish history the eighteenth century is well-remembered as
the century of the Penal Laws. During the previous century, in
post-Reformation Ireland, with the general acceptance by ruling
elites of the legitimacy of repression as a means of eliding dissent, one of the more striking features of the code of anti-
Catholic legislation known as the Penal Laws is its late generation.[4] It was not until after the Williamite Wars ended that anti-
popery legislation was first introduced in 1695.

These laws had considerable effect upon the educational efforts of the Catholic peasantry. Under legislation, Catholics
were barred from going to school or teaching in school.
Likewise, they were restrained from going abroad for education. Strong evidence suggests that these laws were enforced
during the first half of the eighteenth century and that they

---

2. Ibid., p. 37.
3. Ibid.
4. J. Kelly, The Ascendancy and the Penal Laws in J.R. Bartlett and S.D.
Kinsella (eds.), *Two Thousand Years of Christianity and Ireland*, (Dublin:
The Columba Press, 2006), p. 133.

remained a threat for a considerable time thereafter.[5] During the
1780s and 1790s the laws pertaining to a ban on Catholic education were lifted: the Relief Act of 1793 provided that 'persons
professing the popish or Roman Catholick[sic] religion ... shall
not be liable to any penalties ...'[6]

During the lifetime of these laws, and as a consequence of
them, there emerged during the eighteenth century a popular
tradition of schooling which became known as hedge schools.
Although the hedge schools were a rural phenomenon, an
urban version of these schools emerged later. While the penal
laws relating to education seem to have gone off the statute
books with legislative ease, their educational consequences lin-
gered well into the nineteenth century. Over a period of one
hundred and fifty years there emerged a patchwork of schools,
their number reaching at least 9,000 in the 1820s. No other type
of educational institution either before or since reached any-
where near that number. Not only were these schools supported
by the people, but there was a kind of community spirit involving the priest as well. From the 1780s one witnesses the chapel
being used as a school during the week and sometimes before
Mass on Sunday mornings – hence the name chapel school. The
trend during the second half of the eighteenth century, but particularly, following 1782, when the first of the Relief acts was
passed, was to move the hedge school indoors.

Though the bishops generally frowned upon these popular
schools, largely because of the questionable morality of some of
the teachers, at a local level there developed a healthy, coopera-
tive relationship between teacher and priest. The priest welcomed a teacher to the parish and supported him as much as
possible provided some catechism was taught. Despite the fact
that the content of some of the books used in the schools was
often upset the hierarchy, much of the content of the five hundred or so titles used in these schools was also very commend-
able and could be found on the shelves of a gentleman's library.

5. M.Spillane, *Two Centuries of Popular Education: an historical survey of
the educational institutions of Limerick, 1700-1900* (University College,
Cork, 1973, Unpublished M.Ed. Thesis), see Chapter 7.
6. Akenson, p. 45.

In an official government report from the 1820s it is possible to discern that some of these schools catered for both Catholic and Protestant scholars.[7] However, much more common was the denominational nature of these schools. Hedge schools, or to give them their proper title, pay schools, also existed within the dissenting Presbyterian fraternity. The penal laws also deprived dissenting religious groups of access to education – hence, quite a significant number of these schools catering for dissenting religious groups could be found throughout Ireland, but particularly in the northern half of the country. The important point to remember, as far as the education of Catholics is concerned, is that the local priest and the local teacher had engaged in some form of collaborative endeavour long before the national system was established.

The Societies' Schools

During the eighteenth century the established churches of England and Ireland had undergone upheavals of evangelical fervour. These resulted in the emergence of a galaxy of proselytising societies which, at the beginning of the nineteenth century, were sparing no effort in their attempts to wean Ireland from Roman Catholicism by controlling the education of the country's children.

Richly endowed from public as well as private sources, these societies controlled in 1824 no fewer than 2,119 schools catering for 131,105 pupils, as against 422 schools catering for 46,719 pupils controlled by the Roman Catholic clergy.[8] Among the most successful of these pre-1831 schools were those run by the Kildare Place Society whose aim was to educate the poor 'upon the most liberal principles and divested of all sectarian distinctions in Christianity.'

In 1825 the Society claimed to have 1,490 schools under its direction and about 100,000 pupils but gradually the proseltytising character of these schools became more and more obvious and they were stiffly opposed by the Catholic Church. Daniel

---

7. *Second Report of the Commissioners of Irish Education Inquiry,* H.C. 1826-1827, Appendix.
8. C. Hayes, 'The Roman Catholic Church and the Irish National System of Education' in D. G. Mulcahy (ed.) *Proceedings of the Education Conference,* (University College, Cork, 1977), p. 136.

O'Connell had been a supporter of the Society and was, initially, a member, but from the early 1820s onwards serious questions were asked of the Society by people such as O'Connell.

To give the Kildare Place Society its due, however, in educational organisation and method it was in many ways superior to any other similar body at the time in either Great Britain or Ireland. It became, to all intents and purposes, a national system. Much of what had been introduced by Kildare Place was later aped by the National School System following 1831.[9] By the early 1820s Catholics' confidence in Kildare Place had practically disappeared; O'Connell had resigned as a member and there were calls for investigations into its practices particularly with regard to accusations of proselytism. In 1831 the £30,000 set aside for Kildare Place was simply transferred to the new body, the National Board.

The Catholic hierarchy, seeing its own inability to counteract effectively the considered dangerous spread of Protestant schools, looked to the State to do so. Thus, in 1824 the hierarchy petitioned the House of Commons, begging the House, '... to adopt such measures as might promote the education of the Roman Catholic poor of Ireland in the most effectual manner'.[10] It was partly to meet this demand that the government introduced in 1831 the National System of Education which was 'to provide a combined moral and literary and separate religious education', and from which , though denominationally mixed, 'should be banished even the suspicion of Proselytism'.[11]

The National Board

In the autumn of 1831 the government of Earl Grey set out to initiate a new scheme of education for the benefit of the poor in Ireland. The Chief Secretary of Ireland, Lord Stanley, wrote a letter to the Duke of Leinster setting out the principles of the scheme and inviting the Duke to be head of the new National Board of Education. The document, known as the Stanley Letter, became the blueprint for the National System of education. The

---

9. E. Ó hÉideáin, Control in Irish Education in *Iris Hibernia* (Switzerland: Société Académique Hibernia, University of Fribourg, 1961), p. 62.
10. Hayes, p. 136.
11. Ibid.

new system never went to statute and, therefore, remained as an informal provision.[12] The mixed education principle enshrined in the letter was not original. It had been debated and minted for several years, and by several groups and individuals. As recently as 1830, Thomas Wyse, a Catholic from Waterford, had published his plan for National Education, encompassing the principle of united or mixed education where Catholics and Protestants would be educated together.[13] Stanley, as Chief Secretary, was not a member of the Westminster parliament but was invited to present his plan in September 1831. Though Wyse, who was an MP, was sitting only a few seats away during Stanley's speech, he never received the recognition he deserved for devising the most up to date and most comprehensive plan for National Education the previous year.

Nevertheless, the plan went ahead regardless of whose plan it was and seven members were appointed to the National Board of Education. Only two of the exalted members of the Board were Catholic. This, in hindsight, proved to be a major blunder – the country's three main denominations, Established Church, Presbyterian, and Catholic – were simply assigned a mathematical formula affording each a value of equal importance, whereas in fact Catholics accounted for 75 per cent of the population, and in the interests of democratic representation should have had far more than two out of a total of seven members.[14]

12. No proper comprehensive statutory provision was made for Irish primary education. Its provision by the State remained informal, based on memoranda and circulars, until the Education Act of 1998. Minor inroads in this informality had been made from time to time, such as the School Attendance Act 1926. It could be argued that the Constitution of 1937 when giving primary responsibility for the child's education to the family added to the informal nature of the type of education provided by the State.
13. The mixed education or united education principle meant that Catholics and Protestants would attend the same school together for secular and moral instruction to be given by the teacher. Religious instruction, it was planned, would take place outside of normal school hours, and the teacher would not be involved. This instruction could take place in the school or in another building, where the respective clergyman would provide the lessons separately to suit the needs of the respective denominations. To this extent the Stanley and Wyse plan for mixed education was for secular and moral education only and can be described as non-denominational rather than multi-denominational education.
14. Two from each of the main denominations plus the Chairman, the Duke of Leinster.

The Board's most influential members were Anglican, Archbishop Whately of Dublin and Mr Carlisle, patron of the proselytising Bible societies, both of whom were to edit the books for use in the schools. Despite all this the majority of Catholic prelates were willing to accept the System on trial, on the grounds that it created a vast improvement on the existing situation, vis-à-vis the hedge schools and the Protestant society schools. One member of the hierarchy, Bishop Doyle of Kildare and Leighlin (JKL), echoed the reaction of many to the 1831 initiative when he acknowledged that the system, while 'not perhaps the very best which could be devised, was well suited to the especial circumstances'.[15]

Only Archbishop John MacHale of Tuam was a staunch opponent of the National System from its inception. He was a doctrinaire ecclesiastic to whom any vestige of power outside the control of the hierarchy was anathema. But, in the face of overwhelming episcopal tolerance for the new national System, even MacHale refrained from attacking it at first. The initially widespread Catholic support for the system was reflected in the fact that, by 1835, 90,000 Roman Catholic pupils, as against 15,000 Protestants, had been enrolled in the national Schools.[16]

Dean MacNamara of Bruff, in Co. Limerick was one of the clerics who supported the System. For example, he stated in 1835 that the Catholic clergy were altogether favourable to the national schools, while inspector Hugh Hamill, in his report to the Board in 1837, pointed out that although some Catholic priests were not fully satisfied with the National System, they nevertheless gave it their support.[17]

The first sign of impending trouble came when a discussion on the National Schools took place at a meeting of the bishops in 1838 and MacHale, since 1834 Archbishop of Tuam, voiced his strong disapproval of some aspects of the system. He made it clear that he did not intend to allow schools in his diocese to be bound by some of the rules of the National Board. It was from this point onwards that the bishops were beginning to rethink

---

15. Cited in Hayes, p. 136.
16. Ibid.
17. I. Murphy, "Primary Education" in P.J.Corish (ed.) *A History of Irish Catholicism*, (Dublin: Gill and McMillan, 1971), Vol. 5, p. 13.

the mixed education principle. It was also during this period that a major debate was brewing regarding the University Question, and to a lesser extent the provision of secondary education based on the mixed principle idea.[18]

Catholics at least had a system of elementary education which, in spite of many serious objections that could be, and were raised, against it, seemed at least to some degree workable. The Board said it was willing to receive applications from 'Christians of all denominations' and it was prepared to give very special consideration to any joint application from members of different religious denominations. In fact, joint applications were rarely made.[19] By 1850, only 4 per cent of applications for aid had come from joint applications.

What usually happened was that the Catholic parish priest, or Protestant clergyman – where there were children of these denominations in sufficient numbers – applied for help in building a National School or acknowledgement of the worthiness of an existing school to be recognised under the new rules as a National School. In theory at least, these schools were open to children of all denominations and their faith would, the Board hoped, be protected by the principle of 'combined moral and literary and separate religious education,'[20] a principle that caused tremendous difficulty and often sent inspectors scurrying to all parts of the country to investigate complaints.

From the very beginning, the rules governing national schools were being modified to suit Protestant interests. These modifications commenced at the outset of the System with the introduction of Scripture lessons into the secular instruction period, and included the acceptance by the Board of unilateral applications for aid from Presbyterian ministers. Such dabbling with the rules gave MacHale the opportunity of declaring war on the non-denominational system and of declaring that nothing less than separate education for Catholic children would satisfy all the bishops.

The Presbyterians withdrew support for the System but rejoined later when the rules were modified. The Church of

---

18. Ibid.
19. Ó hÉideáin, p. 62.
20. Ibid., p. 63.

Ireland withdrew completely in 1839 and established a separate organisation called the Church Education Society. In many ways such Protestant bickering in the early days allowed, and paved the way, for a Catholic response which had a much longer gestation period, but ultimately brought the mixed education principle to its knees.

The majority of Irish prelates did not concur with McHale's unqualified condemnation of the System. During the ensuing controversy, which was referred to Rome for judgement, eighteen prelates begged the pope not 'to close up to the poor of Ireland this fountain of instruction so necessary to them.'[21] Rome's final decision in 1841 was not to condemn the National System but to leave it to each individual bishop whether to allow the system to be established in his diocese or not. Yet, though the System was not condemned, it was afforded no more than a temporary and suspicious reprieve. The bishops warned that constant clerical vigilance was necessary to ensure that Roman Catholic pupils of National Schools were not robbed of their faith.

Between 1840 and 1860 episcopal opposition to the National System intensified gradually and for numerous reasons. The first of these was that throughout the 1840s the safeguards against proseltytism in the System continued to be abandoned. This was much to the advantage of men like Dr Whately who, in his own words, used the System to 'wean the Irish from the abuses of Popery.'[22] In 1847, for example, the Commissioners initiated what became known as the Stopford Rule.

The effect of this rule was to remove from the teacher and school manager the onus of excluding the pupil from a religious class conducted by a teacher of another denomination, and to transfer this onus to the parent. As a consequence, Roman Catholic children in Protestant-controlled schools were often encouraged by school authorities to be present at Protestant religious instruction. Changes such as this went towards convincing even the least militant Roman Catholic prelates that a mixed education system outside the control of the hierarchy could not be trusted.

---

21. Hayes, p. 137.
22. Ibid.

Major factors in the Church's increasingly strong stand against mixed education were the arrival in Ireland of Dr Paul Cullen in 1850 and the death of Archbishop Murray of Dublin in 1852. Murray had been the most prominent Roman Catholic on the National Board and with his death the System lost its strongest supporter in the hierarchy. Cullen did not condemn the System out of hand because there was nothing there to replace it immediately. He was, however, a strong believer in episcopal prerogatives over the education of the Roman Catholic laity and an unbending opponent of the principle of non-denominational education. He was also a determined enemy of the Board's Model Schools.[23] Under Cullen's influence, the Irish bishops embarked on a determined effort to change the nature of the system from being non-denominational to denominational.

Throughout the 1850s episcopal opposition to the National System was coloured and enhanced by the spread of Ultramontane ideas among the Roman Catholic clergy. Cullen was suspicious of the London government. It had, after all, shown some sympathy towards the 1848 rebellion in the papal states, and had established the state-controlled and non-denominational Queen's Colleges in Ireland. Increasingly under influence of Cullen's suspicions, more and more churchmen began to adopt the standpoint of the diocesan clergy of Dublin 'that education to be the source of blessings must be animated and controlled by religion.'[24]

The nature of the National System's Model Schools, or training institutions, furnished one of the hierarchy's greatest objections to it. These schools, non-denominational in practice as well as in theory, were, unlike ordinary national schools , completely outside local clerical control and were in the words of commissioner Maurice Cross, 'being established as stepping stones between primary national schools,' and the religiously controversial Queen's Colleges. At no time were the Roman Catholic

23. The Model Schools were better equipped than the ordinary National Schools, though they were National Schools. Between 1848 and 1866, 28 Model Schools were built, half of them in Ulster, where Catholic opposition was weakest. These schools were training centres for teacher candidates (trainee teachers). It was in these schools that the young candidates conducted their teaching practice.
24. Hayes, p. 137.

prelates disposed to tolerating the Model Schools. They demanded continually that the Government should recognise that teacher training establishments for Catholics should be denominational and under the control of religious bodies, as was the case pertaining to teacher education in England. This provided a strong vantage point from which the bishops could argue for and demand denominational training colleges.

Between 1850 and 1860 the hierarchy's opposition to the National System intensified, resulting in the welding of the Irish clergy into a common front necessary for effective opposition to it. In 1860 the bishops decided finally that unless their basic demands were met they would break with the system altogether.[25]

The hierarchy's call amounted to demands for de facto denominational education. Its objectives were:

a) to obtain clerical controlled denominational teacher training colleges for Catholics
b) to obtain government recognition that the many primary schools attended solely by pupils of one religion should be classified officially as denominational, and thus freed from all existing restrictions upon religious instruction and practices.

In its struggle to obtain these demands, the episcopacy grew increasingly aggressive. The prelates refused to be pacified when, in 1860, reforms were granted which decreed that Roman Catholics should now make up 50 per cent of the National Board and the Inspectorate , but which left mixed education unaffected. In 1862 the bishops forbade Roman Catholic clerical managers from employing teachers who were trained in the model schools. A year later the hierarchy introduced a ban on Catholic children from attending a National School where the teacher was trained at Marlborough Street or had spent some time in a Model School. Episcopal opposition to non-denominational education was further demonstrated when, in 1869, Cardinal Cullen announced that parents who sent their sons and daughters to Marlborough Street training establishment would be refused the sacraments.[26]

---

25. Ibid., p. 138.
26. Ibid.

It was owing to the persistent efforts of the Roman Catholic episcopal lobby and those of its overwhelmingly loyal laity that the Powis Commission was established in 1868 to consider the National System. Its recommendations in 1870 in favour of Catholic claims declared bankrupt the policy of non-denominational education. These recommendations were implemented over the next three decades and they helped greatly to make inevitable the eventual supplanting of mixed education by unmixed in the system.

Irrespective of the Powis Commission's findings, however, it appears doubtful whether the Government could have withstood indefinitely Roman Catholic demands. Under the guidance of Cullen, the Church had, since the middle of the nineteenth century, developed enormously in a sense of confidence as to its powers and prerogatives. It sought now after its goals, not with timid requests as in penal times, but rather with the uncompromising demands that typified Cullen himself. Encouraged by the Disestablishment Act of 1869 and by Gladstone's Land Act of 1870, Cullen must have felt confident that in a new and more democratic age the Church of the majority would inevitably wield an increased influence over Irish education affairs.

In 1883 the National Board decided to recognise and offer monetary aid to denominational training colleges. The surrender of the Board to episcopal demands on this major issue marked a watershed in the Church's struggle with the System. By 1900 denominational colleges were established and the original Central Training Establishment in Marlborough Street remained as a training institute until 1922, becoming the headquarters of the new Department of Education in 1924. St. Patrick's College, Drumcondra, Dublin,[27] Our lady of Mercy College, Carysfort, Dublin, De La Salle College, Waterford, Church of Ireland College, Dublin, St. Mary's College, Belfast, and Mary Immaculate College, Limerick, gave public utterance to the fact that by end of the century primary education in Ireland had become denominational.

---

27. It had been used as a training college for men under the direct auspices of the Archbishop of Dublin since 1875, but from 1883 was supported by the state as a denominational training college.

At the turn of the century it was still possible to find Catholic and Protestant children sitting side by side in a handful of classrooms. But, by then a system which had started out in the 1830s on the basis of non-denominationalism had by century's end become de facto denominational while still clinging to the principles of a *de jure* notion of united education espoused by a variety of individuals during the early part of the century.

In a pastoral letter issued in 1900, the Catholic hierarchy formally acknowledged the success in remodelling the national school system from the original plan:

> The system of National Education ... has itself undergone
> a radical change, and in a great part of Ireland is now, in
> fact, whatever it is in name, as denominational almost as
> we could desire. In most of its schools there is no mixed
> education whatsoever.[28]

By 1900 it was still possible to find Catholic and Protestant children sitting side by side in a handful of classrooms. But, by then a system which had started out in the 1830s on the basis of non-denominationalism had by century's end become de facto denominational, while still clinging to the principles of a *de jure* notion of united education espoused by a variety of individuals during the early part of the century.

In the early decades of the twentieth century Irish education continued to be plagued by inadequate finance and by unrest regarding remuneration of teachers. In 1918 a committee of enquiry had been set up under the chairmanship of Lord Killanin to report on possible improvements in the status, conditions of service, promotion and remuneration of the teachers in the National Schools and in the distribution of grants from public funds for primary education in Ireland.[29] This report culminated

28. J. Coolahan, "Church-State Relations in Primary and Secondary Education" in J. P. Mackey and E. McDonagh (eds.), *Religion and Politics in Ireland at the Turn of the Millennium* (Dublin: The Columba Press, 2003), p. 133 (Originally quoted in *The Irish Teachers' Journal*, 6th October 1900, 4).
29. P.J. Wall, "The Bishops and Education", *Oideas* 25 (Iris na Roinne Oideachais, 1980), p. 5. Also, J.Coolahan, "The Education Bill of 1919-problems of educational reform" in *Proceedings of the Educational Studies Association of Ireland Conference* (Galway: Galway University Press, 1979), pp. 11-31.

in bitter controversy. Apart from addressing teacher salaries and the amalgamation of small schools, it also brought to the forefront issues which were to prove problematic for the Catholic Church and its perceived role within the management and control of schooling. The report made the recommendation that local committees be established to look after such requirements as school maintenance, repairs, heating, cleaning and the provision of general requisites within National Schools.[30] In order to finance this initiative, a local tax rate should be imposed. This report formed part of what later became known as the MacPherson Bill. Chief Secretary for Ireland, MacPherson proceeded with a bill for Irish education in 1919. The conflict that ensued became the last great Church-State battle. Catholic sensibilities did not agree with arrangements where lay people might have a say in the management of schools. The bishops, including Cardinal Logue, denounced the Bill on the alleged introduction of alien and socialist influences. Under episcopal pressure, culminating in a national novena and petition to be signed by fathers of Catholic families, the Bill was withdrawn in December 1920.

Had it been passed it would have meant better working conditions for teachers and pupils alike: education standards would have had an inevitable improvement; a managerial system which was by then obsolete, would have been revamped in such a way that new innovative European ideas might have been able to gain a foothold in Irish primary schools.

This Bill was proposed on the eve of a type of political independence: while Protestant interests were in favour of it succeeding, Catholic opposition ensured a sectarian division over the issue of education. It was in many ways an excellent Bill and the fears of the hierarchy were largely unfounded. It might have enabled some kind of political unity to be embraced throughout a divided country. A commentator in the *Times Educational Supplement* had this to say: 'Educational unity might have done something to save Ireland from the political partition from which it has already suffered much; at any rate, it would have closed the door on educational extremists.'[31]

30. Following World War I, conditions in Irish schools were deplorable as a result of inadequate funding.
31. Wall, p. 7.

The upshot of this failed initiative was that it would be a long time before a Dublin government would interfere with tradition-al Catholic power and control within the realms of education. 'The Catholic Church had fought and won too many educational battles under the old regime to let its position be undermined, as it saw the situation, during the last gasps of that regime.'[32]

The New State

Under a new government from 1922 onwards one would have expected significant reform in education. A reappraisal of the whole system would have been welcome, and perhaps an at-tempt to increase state control of the system or the involvement of local authorities in its administration.[33] In reality the colonial administrative legacy was maintained and continued with little or no innovative changes.

The Church through the Association of Catholic Managers was already on record as to what it expected from the native government:

> We feel confident that an Irish government established by the people, while safeguarding the material interests of the new state, will always recognise and respect the prin-ciples which must regulate and govern Catholic educa-tion, and in view of pending changes in Irish education we wish to assert the great fundamental principle that the only satisfactory system of education for Catholics is one wherein Catholic children are taught in Catholic schools by Catholic teachers, under Catholic control.[34]

This unambiguous statement set the tone for decades to come: successive ministers for education accepted this inherited status quo. Eoin MacNeill, one of the ministers, declared that the role of the State was one of aiding and assisting agencies such as the churches in the provision of schooling.[35] His successors, John Marcus O'Sullivan and Thomas Derrig, had no difficulty with this understanding. In fact:

---

32. Coolahan, *Church-State Relations in Primary and Secondary Education*, pp. 135-136.
33. Wall, p. 8.
34. Quoted in Wall, p. 8.
35. Coolahan, *Church-State Relations*, p. 136.

Over most of the period since independence, the remarkable feature of educational policy in Ireland has been the
reluctance of the state to touch on the entrenched positions of the Church. This is not because the Church's
claims have been moderate; on the contrary, it has carved
out for itself a more extensive control over education in
Ireland than in any other country in the world. It is because the Church has insisted on its claims with such
force that the state has been extremely cautious in entering its domain.[36]

Church and State were in harmony in the early decades of
the new order. The State accepted that its role in education was
subsidiary to that of the Church, aiding and assisting the
churches in the provision of educational facilities.[37] Following
the Plenary Synod at Maynooth in 1927, the bishops reiterated
the ban on non-denominational education, along with a re-
minder of their approval of the system of clerical managers.

As far as Northern Ireland was concerned, significant por-
tions of the failed Bill of 1919/20 were introduced in a 1923 Bill
which supported the principle of mixed education and where all
schools were to be administered by Local Education Authorities
appointed by Boroughs or County Councils. Therefore, education was to be controlled locally with a division of authority between the ministry and local education authorities. Opposition
to these new arrangements sprang from the bishops: they were
particularly concerned about the banning of religious instruction during normal school hours; equally, the abolition of the
traditional managerial system caused serious unease. Over the
next decade, or so, much of what had been proposed in the Act
of 1923 was withdrawn or amended, Thus, a twentieth century
attempt at non-denominational, non-sectarian education in one
part of the island of Ireland had failed.

The 1960s witnessed the beginning of some rumblings of
change: one possible reason for this, apart from political and
economic ones, was that Pope John XXIII was relatively more

36. J.H. Whyte, *Church and State in Modern Ireland, 1923-1970*, (Dublin:
Gill and Macmillan, 1970), p. 21 (quoted in Coolahan, 'Church-State
Relations in Primary and Secondary Education', p. 139).
37. Wall, p. 9.

liberal than his predecessors and allowed for some greater degree of state intervention in education. Likewise, post-Vatican II Ireland embraced a more humanistic understanding of education. One of the consequences of the shifting sands of the 1960s was the emergence of Boards of Management for primary schools in 1975, replacing the concept of the lone clerical manager. So, since the 70s, some inroads have been made in the traditional managerial grip held by the clergy.

Concluding Remarks

The history of Irish education was fraught with difficulties and squabbling among the various Christian denomination for centuries. It became, essentially, a question of control over the hearts and minds of the Irish poor. During the period of the Penal Laws two distinct education endeavours manifested themselves: one was a popular response to the denial of civil rights to Catholics and dissenters; another, late in the eighteenth century, was the Protestant middle-class provision for a variety of welfare type institutions supported by private and public means, again for the Irish poor. The latter had an ulterior religious motive: these societies, and their schools, were ostensibly proseltysing in nature and in design.

The third decade of the nineteenth century witnessed an increasing political Catholic advance: the Westminster establishment felt, under increasing demands from the likes of O'Connell, that Catholic demands for some form of greater democratic participation might be in the offing. It was in the context of post-Union political debate that a National System of education was offered to Ireland in the 1830s: this had nothing to do with benign benevolence; this was more of a social experiment, undertaken in Ireland, an experiment that could not be countenanced in England, as the middle classes had their own views on who should provide education and who should control it.

Thus, in 1831 it was announced that Ireland would have a National System of education supported financially by the State and managed jointly by members of the various churches. The scenario conjures up an image of a cosy relationship of twin-bedfellows between the churches and the State. This expectation

of intimacy was idealistic and within a decade the plan was beginning to unravel. By 1850, it had come under serious scrutiny
by both Catholic and Protestant churches in Ireland. Twenty
years later, the Treasury was seriously threatening to remove all
financial support for this 'experiment' in Ireland. By then, it was
clear that the Catholic hierarchy had a well-defined agenda of
its own – denominational education and denominational
teacher training institutions.

Catholic leaders had achieved their aspirations by 1900, and
over the next twenty years some attempts were made at introducing local lay management within the primary school sector,
most notably in 1919. Subsequent attempts, between the 1920s
and the 1960s, to address the issue of Catholic dominance over
the primary school system fell on deaf ears.[38]

The 1960s and 1970s witnessed significant changes in Irish
education at almost all levels, including primary. A long-antici-
pated New Curriculum bore fruit in 1971 and lone clerical managers gave way to management boards in 1975. However, the
Catholic Church still held considerable power within Irish
education, as the local priest was, more often than not, the
chairman of the board of management of primary schools.
Notwithstanding that, in more recent times concern has been expressed by Church authorities with regard to the declining
numbers entering the religious life. This phenomenon has consequences for future clerical involvement in primary education
in this country, and no doubt it will pave the way for new strategic paths in the future.

38. See N.Ward, 'The I.N.T.O., The Bishops and the Clash on School
Funding (1945-1954)' in *Irish Educational Studies*, p. 10, (1991). Also, J.
Walsh, *The Politics of Expansion: the transformation of educational policy in
the Republic of Ireland, 1957-72*, (Manchester: Manchester University
Press, 2009).

CHAPTER FIVE

How Catholic Primary School Education is Organised, Managed and Delivered in Sydney, Australia

Kelvin Canavan

The organisation, management and delivery of Catholic schooling in Australia has changed dramatically during the past forty years. Until the early 1960s Australian Catholic schools were relatively autonomous and any links to a diocesan Catholic Education Office (CEO) were tenuous. Deprived of any financial assistance from government, they struggled to accommodate all those seeking places in a Catholic school. But, within the space of forty years, these parish primary and regional secondary schools were transformed and became partners in flourishing diocesan systems of schools, managed by CEOs. Enrolments rose to record levels as immigrants from many countries sought places in Catholic schools.[1]

This paper identifies the factors contributing to the development of the CEO of the Archdiocese of Sydney and provides an overview of its contribution to the educational mission of the Church. In the years ahead CEOs will face a new set of challenges as they help schools respond to a weakening of the Catholic culture and religious practices symptomatic of a more secular society.

The growth of large and influential CEOs during the past forty years has had a significant impact on almost every aspect of the management and organisation of Catholic education in Australia. During this period the structure and character of Catholic schooling underwent permanent change. What had

1 A more detailed treatment of this topic may be found in 'The development of the Catholic Education Office and a system of schools in Sydney since 1965' by Kelvin Canavan and published by the Catholic Education Office, Sydney, (Bulletin 93) in September 2007. http://www.ceosyd.catholic.edu.au/cms/webdav/site/ceosydney/shared/About%20Us/Bulletins/Bulletin%2093.pdf

once been a loose network of self-supporting, relatively autonomous schools, under the control of Parish Priests and Religious Institutes, was gradually transformed into centralised systems that took different forms in different dioceses.[2] Aspects of this transformation may have relevance for any future reshaping of primary education in Ireland.

Historical Overview

The development of CEOs in the late 1960s came at a time when Catholic schools were struggling with enrolment pressure, large classes, a reduced ability to build and staff new schools, rising costs, and negligible government assistance. The Religious Sisters and Brothers, who for the previous eighty years had done most of the teaching and all of the administration, were thinly spread and seeking some relief. Bishops turned increasingly to their Directors of Schools for assistance with planning and the allocation of scarce resources. In many dioceses school finances were centralised, staffing levels and diocesan school fees schedules were established, and responsibility for the payment of teachers' salaries was transferred from schools and parishes to CEOs. For the first time, Catholic communities began dealing with diocesan education offices.

For almost a century Catholic schools had struggled on without any government financial assistance, apart from some Commonwealth support for secondary school science laboratories and libraries and, in New South Wales (NSW), an interest subsidy scheme for loans on school buildings. The breakthrough for Catholic schools in NSW came in 1968, when the NSW State government introduced grants of $12 for each primary school student and $18 for each secondary school student attending a non-government school. At about the same time the other Australian States and Territories began to provide some financial assistance to students in all non-government schools. Initially the grants were modest, but they were sufficient to keep the schools open. In 1970 the Australian Federal

---

2. An account of this transformation may be found in *'The Changing Face of Catholic schools in Australia'* Catholic Education Office, Bulletin No. 88 (May 2006) by Kelvin Canavan.

(Commonwealth) government also began to pay grants to assist with the ongoing recurrent funding of all non-government schools in Australia.

The functions of CEOs were gradually expanded, and by the early 1970s Catholic schooling in the various dioceses began to take on some of the early characteristics of a 'system'. The move towards more structured diocesan administration was assisted by the deliberations at the National Conference on Catholic Education in Armidale in 1972. This conference crystallised a considerable volume of earlier debate on the administrative needs of Catholic education. The Australian Catholic Bishops' Conference then established an expert committee which held its first meeting on 27 April 1973. This committee met on five occasions and its report *'The Organisation of Australian Catholic Education'* was released four months later (Bourke, 1973). The major recommendations were quickly adopted and diocesan, State and national administrative structures were put into place without much delay. These new structures were required if Catholic schools were to maximise the emerging opportunities flowing from the education policies of the recently elected Whitlam government.

True to pre-election undertakings, the Whitlam government lost no time implementing election policies and immediately CEOs were required to manage new programs, including general recurrent resources, school buildings, primary and secondary libraries, disadvantaged schools, Special Education, teacher development and innovation. The establishment of the Australian Schools Commission in 1973 had immediate implications for Catholic schools, and served as both a catalyst and an incentive to hasten the development of suitable organisational arrangements. The Commonwealth government declined to deal with individual schools, leaving the various State and diocesan education authorities to assume responsibility for the distribution of government per capita grants to individual schools, according to need.

To access these new Commonwealth programs, those responsible for diocesan systems of schools were required to have in place administrative procedures that satisfied the program guidelines and accountability demands of the government.

Given the ready availability of considerable funds for immediate expenditure, the CEOs quickly gathered staff to manage the new programs.

The above arrangements, while restricting the direct administrative involvement of the Commonwealth government in individual schools, significantly increased the responsibilities and spheres of influences of the CEOs. In the Archdiocese of Sydney, for example, the CEO in 1969 had a total staff of about fifteen people, predominantly priests and religious, most of whom were part-time due to other responsibilities. By 1979 the staff in the CEO had increased to about eighty, with some salaries paid from Commonwealth Special Purpose programs.

By the end of the 1970s, Catholic schooling in Australia had a very different appearance from a decade earlier. School communities and parishes continued to be highly committed but, for the first time, the schools had the resources that allowed them to respond more appropriately to the needs of students. There was a new confidence in the future of Catholic schooling and increasingly CEOs were giving some shape to this new environment. This growth of CEOs was to continue and, over the next twenty five years, the various CEOs became involved in the delivery to systemic schools of an increasing number of State and Commonwealth government policies and programs. This period was marked by increased government accountability and compliance requirements, as a condition of funding.

This confidence was a tribute to the Religious Institutes, the Bishops and clergy, Principals and teachers, parents and students, and the wider community who had set aside established traditions and practices to re-position their Catholic schools for the decades ahead. They had responded pragmatically to new opportunities in a changed environment. The pace of this re-shaping was breathtaking.

Diocesan CEOs are unique to Australia and their history needs to be told. What follows is a very broad overview of the development of one of these CEOs, told by someone personally involved in the administration of the Sydney Catholic school system since January 1968.

The Beginning of the System in Sydney: 1965-1986

Prior to 1965, Catholic schools in Sydney were relatively independent. Each school raised its own funds, and the Principal or the Parish Priest paid any lay teachers employed. As a response to a financial crisis, a decision was taken in 1965 by Cardinal Norman Gilroy, Archbishop of Sydney, to pool all financial resources and liabilities from all parish primary and regional secondary schools, and to pay teachers' salaries and stipends for Religious from a common fund. A scale of tuition fees for these schools was introduced, and all proposals for additional buildings would require approval. A Catholic Commission was established as the principal decision-making body and Cardinal Gilroy chaired the monthly meetings. The Catholic Education Office (CEO) was a link between the Commission and the schools and became progressively responsible for the management of this new 'system' of schools.

The 1965 decision to begin to centralise and co-ordinate what had previously been a loose network of self-supporting, relatively independent parish primary and regional secondary schools was to change permanently the structure and character of Catholic education in Sydney. In the early 1970s the CEO, Sydney and the Catholic Commission had quickly to assemble staff to manage the emerging system and to allocate government funds to systemic schools according to need. This was a difficult task, as the earlier model of Catholic schooling had not prepared people for these new responsibilities. Bishops, the Diocesan Director of Schools, priests, Religious and lay employees found themselves assessing needs and managing programs that only a few years earlier could not have been imagined.[3]

In 1973 a lay Principal was appointed to De La Salle College, Ashfield and the Diocesan Director of Schools (through the CEO, Sydney) assumed responsibility for his employment rather than the local parish priest. With the coming of the first Industrial Award in 1970 for teachers in Catholic schools in NSW, the CEO, Sydney assumed responsibility for a range of

---

3. *'Worth the Struggle'* (1996) by John Luttrell (published by Catholic Education Office, Sydney, Australia) contains a short history of these developments.

employment-related functions. In a few dioceses, the Parish
Priest continued as the employer of staff working in Catholic
schools. The 1970 Award was significant as it provided Catholic
school teachers for the first time with salaries comparable to
teachers in government schools. The introduction of a superan-
nuation scheme in 1981 and the first Award for Catholic school
Principals in 1989 completed the remuneration arrangements
that allowed lay employees to opt for a long-term career in
Catholic education.

The rapid withdrawal of Religious Principals, particularly
from parish primary schools, had an immediate impact on the
development of the 'systematisation' of Catholic schooling in
Sydney. Between 1975 and 1977 a total of forty-four lay
Principals were required to replace Religious who had been
withdrawn by the Leaders of their Institutes. This took the small
CEO, Sydney and the Catholic community generally by surprise. It demanded a concerted effort to find sufficient lay leaders and to put in place conditions of employment and contract
arrangements. This gradual replacement of Religious Principals
continued and progressively the CEO, Sydney accepted a variety of management responsibilities that had previously been undertaken by Religious Institutes. The need for the professional
development of the new primary lay Principals – and the continuing Religious Principals – became an immediate priority for
the fledgling CEO, Sydney. The Leadership Development
Program launched in 1976 proved to be critical in the preparation of leaders for Catholic schools in Sydney.[4] This program
was subsequently expanded and now extends to teachers interested in future leadership.

During the early 1980s the roles and responsibility of the
CEO, Sydney continued to grow in response to an expansion of
Commonwealth Schools Commission initiatives including a
Participation and Equity program, an English as a Second
Language program, a Multicultural Education program, an
Ethnic Schools program, a Country Areas program and various
professional development programs. The rapid growth in the

---

4. Catholic Schools Leadership Program (2001) delivered by the
Catholic Education Office, Sydney.

roles, services, and structures of the CEO, Sydney and the transfer of considerable authority and responsibility from the priests and Religious to the CEO was characterised by some tension and ambiguity, as those in positions of responsibility struggled to clarify lines of authority and responsibility in the developing system of schools.

By the mid-1980s schools were enjoying the benefits of the steadily increasing government financial assistance: class sizes continued to fall, the Commonwealth's Special Purpose programs were assisting students with particular needs, and teachers were benefiting from professional development programs. Principals were supported by school secretaries, and had considerable relief from day-to-day classroom teaching. Some new schools had opened and others had been refurbished, some courtesy of the Commonwealth Capital Grants Program. Lay Principals for the most part were accepted by the Catholic community and provided strong leadership in changing times.

Archbishop (later Cardinal) Edward Clancy was appointed Archbishop of Sydney in 1983, and early in 1985 authorised 'a wide-ranging review of the structures and procedures within the Archdiocesan system of schools' to be undertaken. In May 1985, a preliminary report confirmed the presence of the organisational weaknesses identified in previous reviews. Concurrently, a doctoral study of perceptions and expectations surveyed all 256 systemic school Principals in the Archdiocese and all 124 CEO professional staff in October 1985. The interplay between people, organisational structures, services and goals to be achieved was examined. The study found:

> The system is characterised by a confusion resulting from an uncertainty of roles and mutual expectations of Principals, priests, the CEO, the Catholic Schools Finance Office and the Sydney Archdiocesan Catholic Schools Board, by discontinuity in structure and goal setting, by tension and by dissatisfaction (Canavan 1986, 28).

The conditions found in the various reports could be readily explained, given the existing network of schools prior to centralisation; the rapid rate of change; the transference of power and responsibility from Parish Priests and Principals to the CEO,

Sydney; the appointment of lay Principals; and the retirement of many Religious Principals and teachers.

The first twenty years (1965-1986) of the expanded CEO, Sydney were characterised by efforts to facilitate new administrative and organisational arrangements to allow systemic schools initially to survive, and then to readjust and begin to flourish in a changed education environment. The next phase (1987-2007) would see the schools benefiting from a more stable and mature organisation.

Consolidation of the System in Sydney: 1987-2009
In April 1986 a decision was made to establish two new dioceses from what was previously the large Archdiocese of Sydney. The new Bishops of Broken Bay and Parramatta appointed Directors of Schools and established separate CEOs in January 1987. At the same time Archbishop Clancy responded to the calls for changes by restructuring the Sydney Archdiocesan Catholic Schools (SACS) Board and the Catholic Education Office.

Under the NSW Education Act 1990 (Part 7, 39-40) the CEO, Sydney 'as the approved authority' is responsible for the operation of the schools in terms of the requirements for Registration and Accreditation of non-government schools. Principals continue to be responsible for the compliance of the school's curriculum with these requirements. The CEO, Sydney has an ongoing responsibility for monitoring school compliance with the NSW Board of Studies requirements. This includes validating the school's Annual Report to the Community. A consequence of the change of governance was that Inspectors of Schools no longer visit Catholic schools. The accountability function was now integrated into the school system as a whole (*School Review and Improvement Framework for Catholic Schools* 2005, 8).[5]

The leadership of the CEO capitalised on the more settled administrative environment by gradually focusing the attention of

5. Catholic schools followed the curriculum mandated by government. In addition, there is a religious education curriculum approved by the Diocesan Bishop. Religious Education is compulsory for all students in Catholic schools. In the Archdiocese of Sydney the government curriculum is complemented by the curriculum support document 'Sense of the Sacred'.

both school Principals and CEO staff on the improvement of classroom practice and student learning. This shift of culture was faster in primary schools than in the larger, more complex secondary schools. Increasingly, the agenda of the CEO moved from administrative and organisational issues to improved educational outcomes in the Catholic tradition. The new leadership team at the CEO, Sydney moved quickly to provide clear strategic direction for the school system. Priorities were established. Principals responded to this lead from the CEO and progressively became more strategic in their own leadership. By 1993 most schools had adopted a cyclic approach to planning and school review. School strategic management plans began appearing and in 1995 a new ten-year strategic plan: *'Sydney Catholic Schools: Towards 2005'* was launched at the Darling Harbour Convention Centre.

In the 1986 study Principals had been ambivalent in their perception of the influence of the CEO, Sydney on classroom instruction. By 2004 the perceptions were different. A doctoral study by Mark Turkington carried out in 2002-2003 reported that Principals and senior CEO personnel perceived the CEO as a learning organisation having a positive impact on standards in Religious Education, literacy, and numeracy.

The initial factors contributing to this change of perception included:

- System-wide priority for improvement in teaching and learning
- Focus on data analysis and reporting school achievement
- Target-setting at school and system level
- Tracking individual student performance
- Student academic achievement in State and National examinations in Years 3, 5, 7, 9, 10 and 12
- Targeted intervention to improve student performance in particular schools
- Reporting achievement against published Key Performance Indicators and targets
- Principals responding to the challenge from the Executive Director of Schools and CEO staff to provide strong instructional leadership and to be personally involved in teaching and learning.

In 2004 a panel of four distinguished educators, including two from the UK, was engaged to evaluate the implementation of the 'Towards 2005' plan and to report on the effectiveness of the CEO and the system of schools. The *Report from the External Review Panel* stated:

> Overall the CEO, Sydney is a highly effective and well-led organisation, characterised by the high commitment of staff at all levels. Its strong Catholic and educational mission adds significantly to the work of systemic schools and to the educational experiences and learning of young people … The CEO, Sydney is proudly and unapologetically Catholic. There is a vibrant and very strong sense of Catholic identity throughout the Sydney Archdiocesan Catholic school system, which is easily evidenced across the Central Office, the Regional Offices and the schools which the Panel visited. (Gamble, Stannard, Benjamin, Burke, 2004, vii and 7).

An outcome of this review was extensive community consultation culminating in the publication in 2005 of a new strategic leadership and management plan *'Sydney Catholic Schools Towards 2010'* and associated indicators of effectiveness. This strategic planning and goal setting framework is perceived very positively by Principals.

Throughout the periods of change outlined above the Religious Education and formation of students continued as 'core business' for the CEO, Sydney. New K-12 Religious Education curriculum documents were developed between 1989 and 1996. This Religious Education curriculum was revitalised by CEO staff and re-launched by Cardinal George Pell in St Mary's Cathedral in December 2003. CEO staff had worked closely with colleagues in the Archdiocese of Melbourne in the production of a revised edition of the *'To Know, Worship and Love'* student textbooks, which was launched on the same day. The new curriculum and student textbooks were well received by Principals, who indicated that the revitalised curriculum was strengthening the teaching and learning of Religious Education across all Years from Kindergarten to Year Ten. They also said that the new textbooks had been well received by students and parents.

For the past decade students in their final year of primary schooling have sat for the Sydney Archdiocesan Religious Education Test. Over the years the test results have shown a pleasing improvement in religious knowledge and literacy (Annual Report 2008, 20).

Between 1976 and 2006 the region encompassing the Archdiocese of Sydney had experienced a steady decline of 42,300 (or 10.5 per cent) in school-age population and a shift of young families to the South West of the Archdiocese. Many Catholic schools in the Eastern suburbs and the Inner West were only half full, while families in the new growth areas could not be accommodated. Working with the clergy and parish communities, the Archdiocese closed or amalgamated sixty-six schools between 1980 and 2006. In the same period thirteen new schools were established in growth areas. Without a strong and well-resourced CEO this shift of resources would not have been possible, and enrolments in the school system would have declined significantly, rather than increasing by 4,900 (or 6.5 per cent) between 1976 and 2006. There is now a significant Catholic education presence in the developing areas of the Archdiocese and land has been acquired for further development.

Catholics made up 25.8 per cent of the total population of Australia at the time of the 2006 National Census. In the Archdiocese of Sydney the comparable figure was 28.5 per cent.

Table 1

Population of Australia: % Catholic

	2001	2006
Australia	26.6%	25.8%
Sydney Archdiocese	29.9%	28.5%

Australian Bishops Conference: Diocesan Social Profile 4

The demand for Catholic education remains strong. Nationally 52.3 per cent of all Catholic students attend Catholic schools, and in the Sydney Archdiocese the figure is 60.3 per cent.

Table 2

Catholic students attending Catholic schools expressed as a %

	2001	2006
Australia	51.8%	52.3%
New South Wales	52.6%	52.8%
Sydney Archdiocese	60.0%	60.3%

Australian Bishops Conference, Diocesan Social Profile 4

Enrolments in Australian Catholic schools reached record levels in 2007 when 690,621 students were enrolled in 1700 Catholic schools. The number of students in Catholic schools has increased every single year since 1985. Enrolments in Catholic schools represent about 20 per cent of all school enrolments. Many Catholic students are enrolled in government and non-Catholic private schools. A recent trend is for Catholic families to delay accessing Catholic schools until their children enter Year 7 in secondary schools. The reasons for this are many and varied.

The enrolment of students of other faiths in Sydney Catholic schools is increasing and is currently 17.5 per cent of total enrolments. In 1973 it was only one per cent. National comparisons are not available.

Table 3

Catholic School Enrolments: Sydney August Census

Students	2000	2002	2004	2006	2008
Catholic	66,622 85.5%	66,685 84.6%	67,410 84.6%	66,739 83.4%	65,877 82.5%
Other than Catholic	11,307 14.5%	12,183 15.4%	12,273 15.4%	13,313 16.6%	13,980 17.5%
Total	77,929	78,868	79,638	80,052	79,857

Australian Bishops Conference, Diocesan Social Profile 4

Again, the reasons for this increase are many and varied (Pascoe 2007 and Croke 2007). In Sydney the decline in the total school-age population has reduced the demand from Catholic parents for places in Catholic schools. These places have been readily taken by students from other faith traditions. A 2008 study of parents with sons and daughters transferring from government primary schools into Sydney Catholic secondary schools found that 'over ninety per cent of parents who switched to the Catholic system are very satisfied or satisfied with their choice' (Laughlin 2008, p. 4). Fifty per cent of these families were from other faith traditions.

Catholic schools are also popular with families from language backgrounds other than English. In more recent years Catholic schools in Sydney have enrolled large numbers of students from a variety of cultural and language backgrounds including Arabic, Vietnamese, Italian, Tagalog, Greek, Spanish, Chinese, Croatian, Portuguese and Indonesian. Significant numbers of refugees from the Sudan and other African countries are now enrolled in Catholic schools in Sydney. These youngsters are typically poor, speak little English, and struggle to integrate into the Australian way of life. The Catholic education option for new arrivals is reflected in current enrolment statistics, with sixty per cent of all Sydney Catholic systemic school students now classified as from a language background other than English. In NSW government schools the figure is 28.1 per cent.[6] Many of these students attend ethnic Church services and some attend ethnic language classes on Saturday.

By the late 1970s the CEO, Sydney, in association with the NSW Catholic Education Commission and the National Catholic Education Commission, had become involved in the politics of government funding for Catholic schools. Initially this involved the protection of funding levels from those opposed, including the NSW Teachers Federation. The education of the broader electorate was essential, and the misinformation provided by opponents of Catholic schools needed to be corrected. The CEO, Sydney regularly prepared print and electronic

6. NSW Department of Education and Training. 2008. *Annual Report 2007: Statistical Compendium*. Sydney: Strategic Planning and Regulation, p. 13.

materials to ensure that the facts about government funding of schools were clearly explained. The CEO involved school Principals in this campaign, and relationships with members of Parliament were fostered.

Catholic schools have progressively become more dependent on government funding. The grants in 2009 represent about eighty per cent of recurrent expenditure. The remaining twenty per cent comes from tuition fees and building levies. Family discounts apply, and there is a long-standing policy that no child from a Catholic family should ever be excluded because of the inability of parents to pay tuition fees.

Nevertheless, the cost to parents of Catholic education continues to rise, and there is a renewed awareness that costs must be controlled if Catholic schools are to be accessible to less affluent Catholic families. During the current global financial crisis Principals have been pro-active in supporting those families experiencing financial difficulties. Student enrolments in Sydney Catholic schools increased in 2009, despite considerable press speculation that enrolments would decline because of the financial crisis and rising unemployment.[7]

While school Principals are anxious to enrol the full spectrum of students, the reality is that many low-income families do not seek admission into Catholic schools. While schools in Sydney do not hesitate to reduce or even waive tuition fees in cases of financial difficulty, the challenge is to encourage parents to approach the school and make known their financial situation. Earlier research found that "the parents' sense of pride and the stigma associated with accepting alternative arrangements regarding school expenses" were among the main factors hindering schools in their enrolment of students from poor families (Johnston and Chesterton 1994, 70).

The effectiveness of the CEO, Sydney that was recognised by both the 2004 External Review Panel, the 2004 and 2007 Australian Business Excellence Awards[8] and three other business

7. *Come to Our Aid* (2008) by John Luttrell (published by the Catholic Education Office, Sydney, Australia) contains a short history of the struggle for government funding.
8. The Australian Business Excellence Awards are presented annually to high-performing organisations.

category awards can be partly explained by the emergence of a shared culture, characterised by good relationships and consistent approaches to school management and leadership and delivery of services. In the development of this culture the personal and professional support for school leaders was a priority, and system processes were complemented by opportunities to gather, to pray and to celebrate. The strength of this school system was greater than the sum of the parts.

One indicator of the effectiveness of the Sydney Catholic school system is the improved student academic achievement in State-wide examinations. There was sustained improvement in literacy and numeracy scores in Catholic primary schools between 1998 and 2008 (Annual Report 2008, 20-23). Test scores were consistently above the State average. In the 2008 national testing program, Sydney Catholic school students performed well above national averages. These results were all the more remarkable given that sixty per cent of Catholic primary students are from language backgrounds other than English. The results have been well publicised to parents and the wider community. Recent evaluations identified the culture of this school system as an important contribution to improved school performance (Canavan 2005, pp. 1-4).

The growth of these Catholic education bureaucracies is a new phenomenon for the Catholic Church in Australia. The continuing challenge is to evangelise the bureaucracy and to maximise the use of the structures to take forward the educational mission. Care must be taken to avoid letting the bureaucratic structures becoming an end in themselves. Recent studies of the CEO, Sydney indicate that Principals view the organisation positively (Annual Report 2008, p. 38).[9]

---

9. Most of the Principals, teachers and support staff are members of the NSW Independent Education Union (IEU). Over the years the leadership of the Sydney Catholic schools system has established positive relations with this union. The IEU has supported many changes to teaching practice and accountability.

The Years Ahead

The initial development of Catholic education systems in Australia administered by CEOs was clearly a consequence of the reintroduction of government financial assistance and the early decision by the Commonwealth not to become involved with individual schools, but rather to have the Catholic authorities distribute recurrent funding to schools according to need. This development was accelerated by the acceptance by CEOs of leadership and administrative responsibilities for more and more schools as Religious Institutes no longer had Sisters and Brothers available to lead systemic schools.

The continuing growth of these CEOs is also directly related to increasing government intervention in education. As a condition of funding, governments now demand compliance on an ever-widening range of matters, and the CEOs need to ensure that all schools are compliant. As a consequence of the NSW Education Act 1990 (part 7:39-40) the eleven CEOs in NSW are the approved authorities for systems of non-government schools and have responsibility for monitoring compliance of systemic schools with the Act.

A continuing challenge for leaders of school systems is to ensure that systemic schools remain connected to local parish communities. The long-term future of these schools is dependent on their continuing connection with the parishes. School and system leaders must resist any moves that would weaken this relationship. The use of the term 'CEO schools' is not helpful, as it can convey the notion that the CEO is a Catholic equivalent of the NSW Department of Education. Rather, parish and regional schools are partners in diocesan systems that continue to be the principal agents for the evangelisation and education of young Catholics in Australia. These systems are able to harvest resources that are then allocated according to need. Schools in need are supported and new communities assisted with the provision of school facilities. CEOs need to provide support and service without stifling initiative or weakening local ownership of the schools. Considerable wisdom and sensitivity is required to achieve the appropriate balance between local and system responsibilities.

Catholic schools in Australia have changed dramatically in the past four decades. The transition from Religious Sisters and Brothers to lay teachers, the reintroduction of government financial assistance, the steady increase in enrolments, and the emergence of strong CEOs and their systems of schools have all had a profound impact on the shape of Catholic education.

Catholic schools are well regarded. There is considerable community confidence in their effectiveness, and demand for places is strong. Paradoxically, the same forty years have seen a weakening of the Catholic culture and a creeping secularism. Many traditional Catholic beliefs and practices are less obvious, and fewer students and parents attend Mass. Some commentators blame Catholic schools for failure to maintain a vibrant Catholic culture and Catholic practices, while others are of the view that the ability of schools to withstand the secularisation of Australian society is limited. The entire Catholic community is challenged by many complex social factors that make Catholicism less cultural than it used to be. World Youth Day 2008 provided parishes, families, schools and CEOs with a unique opportunity to deepen the engagement of young people with Jesus Christ and the Church he founded.

This paper has given a very brief overview of the development of one CEO in Australia and how it has supported the schools through a prolonged period of transition and transformation. This writer believes that the CEO, Sydney has done this well. In the years ahead CEOs in Australia will be called upon to support schools to manage a different set of challenges in an increasingly secular and technologically shaped society.

The radical reshaping of the organisation and management of Catholic schooling in Australia over the past four decades was a courageous response to changing realities in both Church and society. Those with a stake in the future of Catholic schooling in Ireland may find it helpful to reflect on relevant aspects of the Australian experience.

References and Further Reading

Australian Catholic Bishops Conference, 2008. *Diocesan Social Profile: Archdiocese of Sydney.* Australian Catholic Bishops' Conference, Victoria.

Bourke, James. et al. 1973. *The Organisation of Australian Catholic Education: Report of a Committee.* Canberra: Commissioned by Australian Episcopal Conference.

Canavan, Kelvin. 1986. *Perceptions and Expectations of Roles, Services, Structures and Goals of the Sydney Catholic Education Office Held by Principals and CEO Staff.* Ed.D Thesis. University of San Francisco.

Canavan, Kelvin. 2005. *Improving Student Achievement.* Bulletin 84. Sydney: Catholic Education Office, Sydney.

Canavan, Kelvin. 2007. *The Development of the Catholic Education Office and a System of Schools in Sydney Since 1965.* Bulletin 93. Sydney: Catholic Education Office, Sydney.

Catholic Education Office, Sydney. 1995. *Sydney Catholic Schools Towards 2005.* Sydney: Catholic Education Office, Sydney.

Catholic Education Office, Sydney. 2005. *Sydney Catholic Schools Towards 2010.* Sydney: Catholic Education Office, Sydney.

Catholic Education Office, Sydney. 2005. *School Review and Improvement Framework for Catholic Schools.* Sydney: Catholic Education Office, Sydney.

Catholic Education Office, Sydney. 2008 *Annual Report.* Sydney: Catholic Education Office, Sydney.

Croke, Brian. 2007. 'Australian Catholic schools in a changing political and religious landscape' in *International Handbook of Catholic Education.* ed. G Grace and J O'Keefe, pp. 811-833, Dordrecht: Springer.

Gamble, I., Stannard, O., Benjamin, A., Burke, T. 2004. *Report to the Archdiocese of Sydney on the Catholic Education Office, Sydney and the Sydney Archdiocesan Catholic Schools Board. Sydney*: Catholic Education Office, Sydney.

Johnston, Kristin and Chesterton, Paul. 1994. *The Poor and Catholic schools.* Darlinghurst, NSW: Conference of Leaders of Religious Institutes (NSW).

Laughlin, Alan. 2008. *Parent satisfaction: a study of the perceptions of parents enrolling in Sydney Catholic secondary schools*. Bulletin 100. Sydney: Catholic Education Office, Sydney.

Pascoe, Susan. 2007. 'Challenges for Catholic Education in Australia' in *International Handbook of Catholic Education*. ed. G Grace and J O'Keefe, pp. 787-810, Dordrecht: Springer.

Turkington, Mark. 2004. *The Catholic Education Office Sydney as a Learning Organisation and its Perceived Impact on Standards*. Ed.D Thesis. Australian Catholic University, Strathfield.

CHAPTER SIX

The Provision of Catholic Primary Education in Scotland

Roisín Coll

This paper will highlight key features of the current provision of Catholic Education in Scotland. Given its unique situation, the historical context will first be presented, detailing the significant chronological events that led to the establishment of the system. A thorough examination of the provision of Catholic Education in present-day Scotland will follow and potential challenges to its continuation will be explored.

The Historical Context

Much has been written about identity in Scotland and in particular that of the Catholic community (Bradley 2004; Boyle and Lynch 1998; Devine 2000). This community has recently expanded owing to the influx of immigrants from Central Europe and therefore consists of a combination of several ethnic groups with strong Catholic roots. However, despite remaining a minority entity in an increasingly secular country, the Catholic community has a significant presence in Scotland and the Catholic Church has become a well-established institution (Boyle and Lynch 1998). The community has its origins in the survival of the Catholic tradition post-Reformation, but the immigration of Italians, Poles, Lithuanians and Irish has been the major contributing factor. There are a number of longer established Catholic communities in the Highlands and Islands as well as the North East of the country. However, Catholics of Irish origins are the largest segment of Scotland's Catholic community and are concentrated particularly in the West-central region of the country. This influx of Irish Catholics had an impact on the education system and as Bradley (2004) argues, the current Catholic schools system was created as a direct result of this.

When the Irish first came to Scotland they were often subjected to much hostility as was their 'alien and often detested faith' (Bradley 200:20). Indeed, this was not just confined to Scotland but to other parts of the UK. Morris (1998) explains that Catholic communities suffered long periods of 'persecution, repression and social segregation' and that they experienced religious prejudice 'akin to racism' (92). It has been argued that the struggle to survive and thrive in Scotland has resulted in the well-established and strengthened identity of this community to the present day. While it has also been claimed that social and economic change has led to the integration and acceptance of the Catholic community into Scottish society, there still exists a belief that a struggle against discrimination continues since there are entrenched anti-Catholic sentiments in society (Rolheiser 1994). This claim has been well-documented in recent years (MacMillan 2000).

A high proportion of Scotland's teachers in Catholic schools come from this Catholic community situated in the West-Central belt of the country. These Catholic teachers are employed by the state and are part of the Scottish education system, but they work within the Catholic sector of that system, the origins of which will now be presented.

After the Reformation, Catholics were forbidden to attend Scottish schools or to teach in them. The schools were under the strict control of the Kirk (the Church of Scotland) Assembly. Many Catholics who could afford to, opted to send their children abroad to be educated but those who were unable to were required to establish an independent Catholic education system of their own. Resources were very limited but a Catholic education system was devised and maintained without much challenge until the middle of the nineteenth century. It was then that the Catholic population of Scotland increased dramatically owning to immigration, as a result of *an Gorta Mór*, the Great Famine of Ireland. A great influx of Irish travelling to and remaining in Scotland, particularly in the West of the country, had a significant impact on the Catholic education system.

By the late nineteenth and early twentieth centuries, Catholic schools in Scotland were staffed by unqualified, underpaid teachers and served a destitute –and mostly Irish – population.

In 1872 the Government in Scotland wished to establish a national education system and all schools (Catholic, Protestant, Episcopalian) were invited to transfer from Church control to that of the state. Schools would become 'public' but they would have the flexibility on an *'ad hoc'* basis to determine their religious nature if they so wished.

The Catholic Church rejected the invitation to transfer the control of its schools to the state on the grounds that the denominational character of the schools would not be preserved, even with the promise that individual schools retained the right to determine their religious nature if they so wished. The Church found this unacceptable. Their schools were very poorly resourced both financially and academically and indeed would have benefited from the lifting of this burden. However, it balanced this with the guaranteed faith dimension of education that the children were receiving in these schools, something about which the community felt strongly (Coll & Davis 2007). All other schools transferred.

For the next forty-five years the Catholic minority paid general and local taxes but did not avail itself of the state education facilities. The state system expanded and became increasingly more professional while simultaneously, the Catholic sector was wrestling with great financial strains and was battling for survival. The lack of properly trained staff had effects on the level of academic achievement of Catholic children. This changed in 1895 when Notre Dame opened in Glasgow, a Catholic teacher training college. The Catholic system improved but was still far inferior to the state system. Eventually, the government recognised that the Catholic community was being unfairly treated on the grounds of conscience and, after much controversy (O'Hagan 2006; O'Hagan & Davis 2007), the Scotland Act of 1918 was passed, giving Catholic children the same formal educational opportunities found in the nondenominational schools. The schools were to be fully funded and maintained by the state but the Church was given control over the religious education curriculum and the appointment of teachers.

It has been claimed that Scotland stood in distinction from other countries in the world with the passing of this act. The financial burden of Catholic schools was lifted and so the expansion of Catholic Education was able to take place. The whole civic status of young Catholics had been raised, which became evident in the 1930s. Catholic attendance at University increased and Catholics joined the professions – particularly in education, law and medicine.

The 1918 (Scotland) Act provided the basis for quality education for Catholics since their schools were now part of the national system, while allowing the Catholic Church to retain the denominational character of its schools by determining the Religious Education curriculum and being responsible for the approval and appointment of staff. This position has remained unchanged for almost a century.

The Current Situation

It could be argued that the Catholic Church has a very healthy position within educational provision in Scotland. Enshrined in law, Scottish Catholic schools are able to enjoy the benefits of full state funding without conceding their Catholic identity. They are administered in exactly the same way as those in the nondenominational sector, through the local authorities, and are fully accountable to the state in terms of standards, policy implementation, leadership and performance. They are inspected and monitored as are all other Scottish state schools. However, Catholic schools are able to preserve their distinctive identity and faith-based mission since the Church has jurisdiction over the employment of staff in Catholic schools and the content of the Religious Education curriculum – a position that it has enjoyed since 1918.

However, Catholic schools in Scotland today are somewhat different to those that existed at the turn of the twentieth Century. As a result of immigration and the effects of secularisation, Catholic schools now teach children from a range of cultural and religious backgrounds. In addition to those parents who are practising Catholics, parents of children from many ethnic communities choose to send their children to Catholic schools, resulting in some classes being very multicultural. Indeed in a minority of Scottish Catholic schools, the school roll can consist of children from predominantly non-Catholic – or even non-Christian – backgrounds. It is also recognised that of those who are baptised 'Catholic', many children attending such schools come from families where traditional practices are not observed, the most obvious of these practices being Mass attendance.

Approval and Qualification

The Catholic Education Commission (CEC) works on behalf of the Roman Catholic Bishops of Scotland in setting national policy on all educational matters. Its operational agency is the Scottish Catholic Education Service (SCES), which, among other things, works to offer support and guidance to schools and Catholic teachers in Scotland and develop and implement plans for the development of Catholic education.

As a result of the 1918 Education (Scotland) Act, and owing to the Church's control over the appointment of staff, potential teaching staff in Catholic schools must satisfy the Church that they are suitable in 'belief and character' (Great Britain Statutes [1918] Education [Scotland] Act). They are also subject to a stringent approval process. Anyone teaching RE must be an approved practising Catholic (all those teaching in Catholic primary schools fall into this category). Moreover, the Catholic Church requires assurance that all other appointed teachers, whether Catholic or not, are committed to the promotion and support of the Catholic school's mission, aims, values and ethos. Approval therefore is also required for non-Catholic staff. The process involves a reference from a priest (or for non Catholics, a professional) who can testify to the commitment of the individual. At present there are over 7000 approved Catholic teachers in Scotland employed in 403 Catholic state schools.

In addition to being 'approved', there is the expectation that Catholic teachers wishing to teach Religious Education in the Catholic sector obtain their 'Catholic Teachers' Certificate'. This certificate indicates to the Bishops' Conference that an individual is adequately equipped to teach Religious Education in the Catholic school. Teachers in Scotland wishing to gain this certificate usually choose to study their Initial Teacher Education (ITE) course (either four-year undergraduate honours degree courses or a one-year professional diploma) at the Faculty of Education at the University of Glasgow (soon to be changed to the University's 'School of Education'). This institution is the only one in Scotland that has the formal responsibility for providing Catholic teachers for Catholic schools and therefore the Religious Education component of these courses is primarily focused on the Catholic faith. Upon satisfying the subject's academic requirements (which includes being observed teaching RE in a Catholic school), in addition to the Catholic Teachers' formation course, students are awarded the Catholic Teachers' Certificate. The only other way of obtaining this certificate is through CREDL (Certificate in Religious Education by Distance Learning) – a distance learning course offered by the same educational institution.

Relationship with State
The working relationship between Church and state regarding Catholic Education in Scotland has strengthened substantially over the past twenty years, particularly as a result of joint policy initiatives where both have been the major stakeholders (Coll & Davis 2007). The creation of the National 5-14 Guidelines in the early nineties found, for the first time, Catholic Church doctrine being presented and published under the auspices of the Scottish Government (formerly the Scottish Office Education Department) through the creation of the Religious Education guidelines for Roman Catholic schools (SOED 1994). This was not an isolated occurrence. In 2004, the Scottish Government announced another major review of the whole curriculum in Scotland, producing an outline statement of principles and objectives entitled 'A Curriculum for Excellence' (SEED 2004). In May 2008, the CEC and Learning and Teaching Scotland (LTS – the Scottish Government's advisory body on the curriculum) released a set of 'draft outcomes and experiences' on Catholic Religious Education spanning both primary and secondary schooling (LTS, 2008) and again rooted in Church doctrine. These are contained under the following headings or 'Strands of Faith':

- Mystery of God
- Image of God
- Revealed Truth of God
- Son of God

- Signs of God
- Word of God
- Hours of God
- Reign of God

Statements referring to the support that staff will receive in terms of their own professional development further exemplify the endorsement of such material by the Government. Through LTS, it has accepted the Church's request that 'school leadership teams and staff in local authorities support this priority with resources and time dedicated to developing excellent practice in Religious Education' (SCES, May 2009).

The positive working relationship that the Scottish Government and Catholic Church seem to enjoy was further endorsed in 2008 by Scotland's First Minister, Alex Salmond when, at the annual Cardinal Winning Lecture – hosted by the Religious Education department at the University of Glasgow as part of the yearly Catholic Education Week initiative – without reservation, 'celebrated' Catholic schools in Scotland and concluded that they 'will always have my support and the support of my government' (Salmond 2008). In this landmark speech he commented:

> I am proud to join with you in celebrating the particular contribution of Catholic schools to our society, to our education system, and to this country. I use the word 'celebrate' quite deliberately ... It is time to celebrate diversity and distinctiveness and to openly welcome the contribution that faith based education can make to Scottish education. From today's perspective, we can see the Education Act of 1918 as a huge positive step in the history of this nation of Scotland. I see every reason to expect us to be celebrating its full century in another ten years' time. I look forward to many more years of successful partnership between us (Cardinal Winning Lecture, 2 February 2008.

This relationship has no doubt been strengthened by the creation of the Scottish Catholic Education Service (SCES).

New Horizons: Challenges for the Future

Opposition
There are obvious challenges to the future and effective provision of Catholic Education in Scotland. One such challenge is the deep-rooted opposition of many political, educational and academic commentators and journalists to such schools (an opposition that could be considered a phenomenon in its own right). The well-rehearsed arguments that have appeared in the Scottish press or wider media – and which often form the basis of debate at grassroots level – continue to appear, despite the Church's endeavors (and those of individuals having a very different political, educational or academic mindset) to present Catholic Education as a positive choice for parents, and essential for the holistic development of the Catholic child. Typically, arguments against the provision include:

- Catholic schools are divisive
- Catholic schools cause sectarianism
- Catholic schools should not be funded with taxpayers money
- Modern Scotland is very different from the Scotland of 1918
- Catholic schools indoctrinate and brainwash children who should be allowed to choose their own faith when older
- Catholic schools discriminate against non-Catholic children and non-Catholic teachers

The Church in Scotland continues to respond to such arguments, (for example, highlighting that Catholic schools exist worldwide – including England, where there are no such sectarianism issues – demonstrating that the Catholic school is not the problem). However such responses, coupled with any high profile endorsement of the Catholic schools' provision (such as Salmond's address in 2008), have been used to provide the protagonists with additional ammunition to present a case for their abolition. The debate continues but the reduction in Church attendance and the claimed growth of secularization has been used to strengthen their argument, even at a time when Catholic schools are bursting at the seams.

From the 'religious' to the 'lay Catholic' teacher.

Another challenge to the effective provision of Catholic schools in Scotland is, what is being referred to here as, 'the changing face of the Catholic School'. No longer do Scottish Catholic schools have clergy or 'religious' teaching within them or indeed, leading them. These responsibilities have fallen to the lay Catholic teacher and this has associated challenges. In the past two decades the Catholic Church has expressed the view that 'all too frequently lay Catholics have not had a religious development that is equal to their general, cultural and most especially professional development' (Sacred Congregation for Catholic Education 1982: No 60). Again this claim has been echoed in the most recent of Church documents on Catholic education where the encouragement of a journey of formation for the lay Catholic teacher is one of its main points of focus (Sacred Congregation for Catholic Education 2007). It can be argued that the main reason for this spotlight on faith development is sociological since the presence of religious teaching orders has diminished in Catholic schools in Scotland, almost to vanishing point (Fizpatrick 2001). There was an inbuilt assumption that the charism of these orders would pass to less experienced lay colleagues who worked alongside the Religious teachers and while this did happen, it has faded out over the generations (O'Hagan 2006). Most lay teachers do not have the same theological knowledge and understanding or spiritual development and devotion that Religious teaching staff acquired by virtue of their life-long formation, vocation and commitment. Indeed as new generations of lay Catholic teachers emerge, their understanding of their spiritual role, and articulation of this, in addition to their adherence to the traditions of their faith have come into question (Coll 2009). In Catholic schools in Scotland today most teaching staff *are* lay Catholics and the Church recognises that the future preservation of the distinctive religious character of its schools depends on these very people.

The Catholic School as Church

It has been recognised (Coll 2009) that the Catholic school is sometimes the only place where Catholic children will receive any religious formation or knowledge about their faith. The traditional catechetical trio of home, school and parish has weakened substantially and the Church now recognises that the school is sometimes the only place where a child will receive an experience of 'Church'. Of course, this is not a particularly Scottish phenomenon but the ramifications of this for the Catholic teacher in the Scottish Catholic school are significant. Parents choosing to send their children to the Catholic school in Scotland do so for a variety of reasons; their proven academic record; their location; their association with an Irish-Catholic identity; another far from insignificant reason is to provide for their children sound moral teachings, steeped in the Catholic tradition, since, often, they cannot provide for this themselves or they live a lifestyle that is at odds with what they fundamentally believe to be good. The expectation of the 'approved' Catholic teacher is therefore heightened and, arguably, more demanding since it can be on their shoulders alone that the responsibility of providing such grounding in morality and faith is placed. In fact in some classrooms teachers find their role to be more of an 'evangelist' than 'catechist' (Coll 2008). This reality brings the disposition of the Catholic teacher into the spotlight.

A New Generation of Catholic Teacher

In a recent study (Coll 2008), thirty newly qualified Catholic teachers in Scotland were tracked over a period of time, from the final year of their study to full registration as qualified Catholic teachers, incorporating a probationary year. The focus of the study was their faith positions and development of their faith. Among many things, the study revealed that a new generation of Catholic teacher in Scotland now exists: one that is still committed to Catholic Education and to accompanying and supporting children on their faith journey but one that lacks knowledge and understanding of key elements of their own faith. Grace (2002:237) has attempted to explain this by referring to a weakening of the Catholic teacher's 'matrix of sources of spiritual capital', where family background, prayer life and mass attendance in addition to experiences of Catholic schooling no longer have the same influence in the lives of Catholics as they once did. A significant finding of the study, however, was the positive impact that the Catholic school environment has the potential to have on a teacher's faith and knowledge and understanding of it, even to the point of transformation. Many of those participating, who were teaching in Catholic schools with a strong identity and effective Catholic leadership, recorded an impact on their own faith position (Coll 2009). One such example was that of Maria:

> There's such a good sense of community in this school. You know, from your line manager, from your mentor and from the head teacher and I suppose you look at the Head and you look at the way the head teacher is and how he cares about the school, those within. It's quite, it makes it quite important to you that you do the same ... You know, my own faith had just kinda dwindled away really and at that point I thought, well I don't want to go into an ethos where people are very religious and I feel out of that or feel under pressure to take more part in it. Actually the opposite happened. I just felt very included when I came in and there was no pressure on me as a teacher you know. I have chosen to become involved in the kind of spiritual life in the school because it is good, you know by helping out if there are retreats etc. Being in this school has actually changed me and I think it definitely has changed my faith. You know I think I grew up with a feeling of guilt since I wasn't really practising. Now it's just a feeling that I go to mass because I want to be there. That's really liberating for me. And that I actually really love that ethos within the school. And I do feel that it has a major impact on me and in turn, on the pupils (Coll 2008:156).

Janssens (2004:147) writes of teachers' 'personal frames of reference' and how these have the potential to be changed and influenced positively or negatively by others. He claims that teachers in the same professional environment discussing and sharing their own frames of reference can result in *shared* frames of reference which can ultimately influence the organisational culture of the school. Flores (2004) supports this highlighting that schools are not only places where teaching occurs, but they are places where teachers learn and develop and that the key to maximising the potential for this is the direction of the school leader. The evidence from Coll's study of Catholic teachers reveals that this is true in the Catholic schools context in Scotland. Where there was a strong Catholic identity and shared Catholic leadership, newly qualified teachers recognised this, responded to it and spoke of its impact on their own faith identity and disposition.

This has clear implication for Catholic school leadership.

Suggestions

This paper has presented the historical origins of Catholic Education in Scotland, the present day reality and the potential challenges to its future. From this emerge a number of related considerations for those responsible for its continued provision:

- Catholic schools leaders should receive dedicated development sessions focusing on the impact that their leadership and direction (verbal and non-verbal) can have on the *teacher*. The nature of Catholic leadership should continue to be explored with every Catholic headteacher.
- All Catholic teachers should be given dedicated time for their own *faith formation*.
- This *faith formation* time should be formally recognised as Continuing Professional Development by the Government.

It is recognised that while these recommendations are directly concerned with the Scottish Catholic schools context, Catholic schools worldwide may benefit from their consideration.

'Remember your leaders ... Consider the outcome of their way of life and imitate their faith' (Hebrews 13:7).

REFERENCES AND FURTHER READING

Boyle, R. & Lynch, P. (1998). *Out of the ghetto: The Catholic community in modern Scotland*. Edinburgh: John Donald.

Bradley, J., ed., (2004). *Celtic Minded: Essays on religion, politics, society, identity and football*. Argyll: Argyll Publishing.

Coll, R. (2008) *Nemo dat quod non habet*. Unpublished Doctoral Thesis. University of Glasgow.

Coll, R. (2009) *Catholic School Leadership: exploring its impact on the faith development of probationer teachers in Scotland*. International Studies in Catholic Education. Volume 1 (2).

Coll, R. & Davis, R.A. (2007) *'Faith schools and state education: Church-state relations and the development of the 5-14 Religious Education program in Scotland'*. Catholic Education: a journal of inquiry and practice, 11 (1), pp. 67-82.

Devine, T. (2000) *Scotland's shame: Bigotry and sectarianism in modern Scotland*. Edinburgh: Mainstream Publishing.

Fitzpatrick, T. (2003) 'Catholic Education in Scotland' in T. Bryce and W. Humes (eds) *Scottish Education: Post Devolution. Second Edition*. Edinburgh: Edinburgh University Press.

Flores, M.A (2004) 'The impact of school culture and leadership on new teachers' learning in the workplace'. *International Journal of Leadership in Education* 7 (4), pp. 297-318.

Grace, G. (2002) *Catholic Schools: Mission, markets and morality*. London: Routledge Falmer.

Great Britain Statutes (1918) Education (Scotland) Act.

Janssens, S. (2004) 'Doctrine versus personal frame of reference' in H. Lombaerts & D. Pollefeyt (eds) *Hermeneutics and Religious Education*. Leuven: Uitgeverij Peeters.

LTS (2008) *Religious education in Roman Catholic schools* at http://www.ltscotland.org.uk/curriculumforexcellence/outcomes/re rc/index.asp (last accessed 02/03/10).

MacMillan, J. (2000) 'Scotland's shame' in T. Devine (ed) *Scotland's shame: Bigotry and sectarianism in modern Scotland*. Edinburgh: Mainstream Publishing.

Morris, A.B. (1998) 'By their fruits you will know them: distinctive features of Catholic education'. *Research papers in Catholic education*, 13 (1), pp. 87-112.

O'Hagan, F.J. (2006) *The Contribution of the Religious Orders to Education in Glasgow during the period 1847 –1918*. Lampeter: Edwin Mellen Press.

O'Hagan, F.J. & Davis, R. (2007) 'Forging the compact of Church and state in the development of Catholic education in late nineteenth-century Scotland'. *The Innes Review*, 58 (1), pp. 72-95.

Rolheiser, R. (1994) 'Mourning a wise critic'. *Catholic Herald*, April 29.

Sacred Congregation for Catholic Education (1982) *Lay Catholics in Schools: Witnesses to Faith*. London: Catholic Truth Society.

Sacred Congregation for Catholic Education (2007) *Educating together in Catholic schools*. London: Catholic Truth Society.

Salmond, A. (2008) *Cardinal Winning Education Lecture, University of Glasgow* at http://www.scotland.gov.uk/News /This-Week /Speeches/ First-Minister/cardwinlecture (last accessed 02/03/10).

SCES (Scottish Catholic Education Service) at http://www.sces.uk.com (Last accessed 02/03/10)

SOED (1994) Religious Education 5-14 Roman Catholic Schools SCEC, Glasgow.

SEED (2004) *A Curriculum for Excellence – The Curriculum Review Group* at http://www.scotland.gov.uk/Publications/

CHAPTER SEVEN

Providing Catholic Primary Education in Ireland: The Patron's Perspective

Bishop Leo O'Reilly

It is a very timely opportunity for us in the Church to reflect more deeply on our vision for Catholic education from different perspectives, parents, teachers, management and patrons. It is especially appropriate, at a time when we are becoming more conscious of the responsibility of the entire people of God for the provision of Catholic education, to do so under the banner of Catherine McAuley who was a pioneer as a lay person in the provision of Catholic education for those who were vulnerable and could not otherwise afford it.

THE EDUCATION SYSTEM

i) Role of Patron Bodies

Our primary education system in Ireland is unique in that, up to now, the State has not generally been a direct provider of primary education. The Constitution, as is well known, puts an obligation on the State to provide for education, rather than to provide it directly. The State has fulfilled this role by providing funding to individuals or groups, known as Patrons, who take responsibility for the actual provision. The Catholic Church, as the representative of by far the largest religious denomination, is also the Patron of the vast majority of primary schools (2899 out of 3282 catering for 92 per cent of primary school children). There are many other Patron bodies, the Church of Ireland, Foras Pátrúnachta, Educate Together, the Jewish Community, and more recently the Muslim Community and the VEC. The latter is the newly appointed Patron Body for Community National Schools, the Additional Model announced by Minister Hanafin a couple of years ago. In speaking about 'The Patron's Perspective', I would not presume to speak on behalf of the other Patrons or Patron bodies. What I have to say will be from the point of view of a Patron of Catholic primary schools.

ii) Safeguarding Children

The reports from various commissions of enquiry over recent years are to be welcomed, even if the litany of abuse perpetrated on the most vulnerable of the vulnerable makes for appalling reading. Children are to be loved and cherished and the Church's failure to protect those in its care was a shameful betrayal of a sacred trust. Establishing the truth of what happened is crucial and the reports contribute to that goal. Victims deserve justice and support to help bring about healing.

An issue that has been raised in the media a number of times in recent times is whether society should 'look to change a system where so much of the educational and care provision for our children is farmed out to organizations who are unaccountable ...' This is not true. School Patrons, whether Catholic or otherwise, are fully accountable to the law of the land. And that is as it should be. I want to state clearly that the safety and welfare of pupils in our schools is assured by State law and regulation. The standards that operate to safeguard children in our schools are those contained in the State's own *Children First: National Guidelines for the Protection and Welfare of Children*, and in relevant legislation, and not those of an individual school patron. So that there can be no ambiguity on this important issue, let me state again: the State's child protection standards apply to all schools and they require that each school have its own Designated Person to receive and report complaints. That person must be a member of the school staff.

iii) Responsibility and Resources

As a Patron Body we clearly have an enormous responsibility in the provision of primary education within the education system. We take that responsibility very seriously and have put huge resources into exercising it. The resources that are most easily quantifiable are financial. The most obvious of these are providing sites for schools and substantial local contributions to all capital projects, but there are lots of other less visible financial subsidies provided by the parishes for our schools. However, the greatest resources provided to education have been the clergy, religious and lay people who have managed schools for generations. Recently this is even more evident in the many committed people, recruited at parish level, who serve on boards of management without even receiving out of pocket expenses.

POSITIVE EXPERIENCE OF PATRONAGE

i) Catholic Ethos

Overall, the experience of providing primary education from the point of view of Catholic patrons has been, I would say very good. We have had the freedom to establish and run schools that have a Catholic ethos. Of course these schools are governed by the Education Act and must comply with all the requirements of the Act in relation to curriculum, standards, inspection, and management which are laid down there. Nevertheless, within those parameters, our schools have the freedom to provide religious education and formation for Catholic students in accordance with the teaching, practices and tradition of the Catholic Church. Their educational philosophy is rooted in the Catholic vision of education which is inspired by belief in God and modelled on the teaching and life of Jesus Christ. Each school aims at promoting the full and harmonious development of all aspects of the person of the pupil: intellectual, physical, cultural, moral and spiritual, including a relationship with God and with other people.[1]

ii) State Support

Catholics in other countries look at our system and marvel at the fact that the State pays almost the entire cost of capital expenditure on new schools. It pays capitation and other grants towards the cost of day-to-day running of the schools, and also pays the teachers' salaries. Of course it does the same for schools of other patron bodies as well. Compared to a country like the U.S., where the State makes no contribution at all to Catholic schools, or schools of any other denomination, our system is very supportive.

iii) Neutral Ethos?

There are some who would argue that the U.S. system should

---

1. Schedule to Deed of Variation for Catholic Primary Schools in Catholic Primary School Management Association, Management Board Members' Handbook, revised edition, (Dublin: Veritas, 2007), pp. 14-18.

apply here. They say that it would be better for schools to keep a neutral stance in relation to religion. They say religion is a matter of personal choice and should be kept in the private sphere. However, it has been pointed out frequently that those who would exclude religion from the school also impart a worldview, a philosophy of life, just as much as the person of faith. Schools that exclude religious instruction are not neutral in their stance. Joseph Dunne has argued very persuasively 'that "ethos" is not a rarefied "extra" that some schools might seek to cultivate on a discretionary basis but rather an unavoidable characteristic of any school ...' [2]

The Catholic philosophy of education maintains that education is for life and religion is, for most people in Ireland, an important part of life. Others embrace a philosophy of life which excludes religion. We respect their freedom to do that, but we do not believe that they should be allowed to impose their worldview on everybody. There is need for pluralism of provision – within reasonable limits – so that parents have a choice as far as possible about what kind of school their children will attend. This is a right enshrined in the Constitution, in the Universal Declaration of Human Rights, in United Nations and European legal instruments. Besides, having a non-denominational State education system for everybody would mean that Catholics, and others who wanted a different kind of education for their children, would not only have to pay for the education of their own children through fees, but would also have to subsidise those in the State system through their taxes. That would be double taxation and would be unjust.

CHALLENGES OF PATRONAGE
i) Increasing Complexity of Management and Patronage Functions
We have moved fairly quickly from a situation where there was practically no legislation impinging on the area of primary education to a position where there are now several major pieces of legislation that affect the daily life of schools. The Education Act 1998 is of course the most important of these and it has helped

---

2. In Eithne Woulfe and James Cassin, eds., *From Present to Future: Catholic Education in Ireland for the New Century*, (Dublin: Veritas, 2006), p. 211

bring definition and clarity to many areas which were unclear before. I list below a selection of the other Acts which have a direct impact on the running of schools:

- Employment Equality Act 1998
- Education (Welfare) Act 2000
- Equal Status Act 2000
- Teaching Council Act 2001
- Education for Persons with Special Educational Needs Act 2004
- Education (Miscellaneous Provisions) Act 2007

All of this has made the provision and running of schools a much more complex undertaking than it was previously. It makes extra demands on Patrons who have the considerable burden of appointing boards, approving the appointments of teachers, approving and providing oversight of capital projects, planning future provision, providing training and formation for trustee representatives on boards and assessors for selection boards and a host of other duties. It makes extra demands on boards of management and requires that they have very high levels of competence and training in order to discharge their responsibilities effectively.

ii) Increasing Diversity in Society
A new emphasis in the vision of the Catholic school is the emphasis on inclusivity. The Pastoral Letter, *Vision 08*, captures this emphasis succinctly when it says:

> Catholic education values tolerance and inclusiveness ...
> [It] is open to generous dialogue with Christians of other traditions and those of other faiths and none ... The presence of children from other denominations is seen as an enrichment of the educational experience offered by the school ... The schools see such diversity as offering opportunities for deeper understanding among people holding diverse convictions.[3]

The increasing diversity of our society and the presence of children from many different faiths and backgrounds in our

3. Irish Catholic Bishops' Conference, *Vision 08: A Vision for Catholic Education in Ireland*, (Dublin: Veritas, 2008), p. 8.

schools is seen as something which can contribute to the quality of education being offered to our children. However, coping with the practical demands that this makes in the day-to-day life of the school, does provide challenges to our teachers and boards of management. As Patrons we must support our teachers and boards in providing assistance and guidance in how to teach the Catholic faith and maintain a Catholic ethos, while continuing to respect and make provision for people of different religions and none. The economic downturn in the past year has added to the mix, giving rise to economic constraints on provision and also questions being raised about the feasibility of making separate provision for different groups on religious, linguistic or other grounds.

iii) Underfunding

The quality of our primary education system has been widely and rightly recognised and applauded. At the same time it has often been noted that as a country we spend a smaller percentage of GNP on education than almost any other country in the OECD. I have never seen any attempt to analyse the reasons why we have managed to achieve such high educational standards at such low cost. Up to fairly recently all sites for new schools were provided by the Patrons. I wonder could the main reason be that the costs to the State of management and patronage have until now been negligible in the case of primary schools? However, that situation is unsustainable in the long term. The increasing complexity of the legislation that impinges on schools and education, and the greater awareness among people generally of their rights and their children's rights make it imperative that the functions of Patronage and Management of primary schools are adequately resourced by people who are professionally trained to carried out these duties. The patronage and management functions of the state-run sector at second level – the VEC sector – are carried out by the offices of the Vocational Education Committees. They are appropriately staffed and funded to do this work. It is only right that similar funding and staffing were available to the other patron bodies.

i) The Reason for Church Involvement

Ultimately, the reason for the Church's involvement in education is that we see it as a central part of its mission. It is part of
the commission given by the Risen Christ to the apostles: 'Go,
make disciples of all nations, baptising them in the name of the
Father and of the Son and of the Holy Spirit, and teaching them
to obey everything that I have commanded you' (Matt. 28:18).
The Catholic vision of education sees it as consisting of much
more than simply imparting knowledge to students, or equip-
ping them for examinations, or even preparing them for future
employment. It recognises the importance of these matters but
does not consider them the most important elements of the educational process. In the Catholic vision of things, education is
primarily a moral and spiritual enterprise. It is holistic in its approach and seeks to ensure the harmonious development of the
whole person, body, soul and mind. So it is concerned not only
with the intellectual and physical development of the students,
but with their moral, spiritual and social development as well. A
central part of it is education and formation in the faith. I have
already mentioned how much we value the freedom to do this
in our schools, and how important it is for us that this freedom is
protected and guaranteed in our education system.

ii) Guarantee of Religious Ethos

This freedom was guaranteed in the past by the fact that the
Patron appointed the Manager of the School, and the Manager
of the school was accountable to the Patron for promoting and
upholding the school's ethos. When Boards of Management
were introduced in the mid-seventies this freedom was guaranteed by the provision that the Patron could nominate half the
members of the board, giving him a voting majority should it be
required in order to protect the Patron's interest. In 1997, the
government of the day was anxious that there should be greater
democratic representation on the boards and asked the Patrons
to forego two of their places on the board to facilitate this. This
left the Patron with two nominees on a board of eight members.
In exchange for losing their voting majority on boards the
Patrons were given a guarantee designed to copper-fasten the

ethos of their schools. This was in the form of an amendment to the school lease. The original lease already included an undertaking that the school would be managed in accordance with the Rules for National Schools. The new document, which supplements the original lease, provides that the school will be managed in accordance with the rules laid down by the Minister for Education and in accordance with a Roman Catholic ethos. This was called a Deed of Variation.[4]

iii) Recent Developments Concerning Deed of Variation

The Minister was to be a signatory of the Deed of Variation. Not that the Minister was being asked to uphold the ethos of the school. That is not his responsibility. However, his signature would guarantee the Patron's right to uphold the ethos. This was accepted by all parties in good faith and Patrons set about the difficult task of having all the deeds of their schools so amended. However, somewhere around 2004 I think, the Minister stopped signing the deeds.

This decision seems to have resulted from the advice of Senior Counsel engaged by the Chief State Solicitor which indicated that there is no statutory basis for the Minister to sign such deeds and that provisions within them could be contrary to the Constitution, in particular Article 44.2.5 which provides that religious denominations have the right to manage their own affairs. The object of this article is to guarantee the autonomy of individual religious denominations and to make sure that they are kept free from State interference or entanglement. The Department claims it is now willing to agree an alternative mechanism that will meet the same objectives.

However, this is clearly a cause of great concern to us as Patrons. The agreement entered into in good faith, and the guarantees that went with it have been unilaterally withdrawn. It does raise the question as to whether the freedoms we have enjoyed up to now in relation to the upholding of the ethos of our schools will continue to be guaranteed into the future. And it raises the further question: if such a formal agreement, made in good faith can be changed without consultation then what of other past agreements or of the prospects for future agreements?

---

4. Cf. Management Board Members' Handbook, p. 14.

iv) European Directive

Another concern that we have as Catholic Patrons relates to what is referred to as the European Directive. In October 2000, at a meeting of the Employment and Social Policy Council chaired by France's Martine Aubry, the Council reached unanimous political agreement on the proposal for a Directive establishing a general framework for equal treatment in employment and occupation. However, two amendments were secured in the European legislative process: one by the British Government, which became article 15 of the Directive[5], headed 'Northern Ireland', and dealing with the police, but also with Catholic schools; the other by the Irish Government, greatly extending what became article 4 ('occupational requirements'),[6] designed to exempt discrimination by religious bodies throughout the European Union.

In 2008 the European Commission published a new draft directive intended to combat discrimination in the provision of goods and services. It is known as the 'Equal Treatment' directive. The original version of the directive gave rise to fears

5. Article 15
Northern Ireland
i) In order to tackle the under-representation of one of the major religious communities in the police service of Northern Ireland, differences in treatment regarding recruitment into that service, including its support staff, shall not constitute discrimination insofar as those differences in treatment are expressly authorised by national legislation.
ii) In order to maintain a balance of opportunity in employment for teachers in Northern Ireland while furthering the reconciliation of historical divisions between the major religious communities there, the provisions on religion or belief in this Directive shall not apply to the recruitment of teachers in schools in Northern Ireland in so far as this is expressly authorised by national legislation.

6. Article 4
Occupational requirements
i) Notwithstanding Article 2(1) and (2), Member States may provide that a difference of treatment which is based on a characteristic related to any of the grounds referred to in Article 1 shall not constitute discrimination where, by reason of the nature of the particular occupational activities concerned or of the context in which they are carried out, such a characteristic constitutes a genuine and determining occupational requirement, provided that the objective is legitimate and the requirement is proportionate.

among religious organisations about its implications for religious freedom. For example, what would be the implications for faith-based schools? Education is a service. Would, for example, faith-based schools be forced to admit children not of the faith of the schools and refuse admission to children who are of the school's faith, in a situation where school places were limited?

The Commission of the Bishops' Conferences of the European Community (COMECE) is the official representation of the Catholic bishops of Europe in Brussels. It has proposed amendments to the Commission's draft of the directive. COMECE'S suggestions are intended to properly protect religious freedom against certain interpretations of equality and non-discrimination which pose a threat to religious freedom.

However, the European Parliament (EP) has passed amendments of its own which make religious freedom subject to the principle of non-discrimination. Its amendments weaken the protections for religious organisations and believers contained in the Commission's draft, a draft which, according to COMECE, needed to be strengthened in any case. The EP's amendments have potentially very serious implications for religious organisations as well as member-state family law.

---

ii) Member States may maintain national legislation in force at the date of adoption of this Directive or provide for future legislation incorporating national practices existing at the date of adoption of this Directive pursuant to which, in the case of occupational activities within churches and other public or private organisations the ethos of which is based on religion or belief, a difference of treatment based on a person's religion or belief shall not constitute discrimination where, by reason of the nature of these activities or of the context in which they are carried out, a person's religion or belief constitute a genuine, legitimate and justified occupational requirement, having regard to the organisation's ethos. This difference of treatment shall be implemented taking account of Member States' constitutional provisions and principles, as well as the general principles of Community law, and should not justify discrimination on another ground.
Provided that its provisions are otherwise complied with, this Directive shall thus not prejudice the right of churches and other public or private organisations, the ethos of which is based on religion or belief, acting in conformity with national constitutions and laws, to require individuals working for them to act in good faith and with loyalty to the organisation's ethos.

It is now up to the Council of Ministers whether to pass this directive at all, and in what form. It is urgent to ensure that the Directive, if passed, will properly protect religious freedom.

PATRONAGE: THE FUTURE

i) Need for Adequate Provision

Historically, the Catholic Church has been the provider of the great majority of primary schools in the State because of its position as the Church of the great majority of the people. However, that situation has changed and continues to change. We are now providing primary education for 92 per cent of the population even though the proportion of those in the population who describe themselves as Catholics has fallen to 87 per cent. If we take into account those who are simply nominal Catholics and who may not wish to have their children educated in a Catholic school, and those who, while continuing to be attached to the Church, would choose to send their children to schools under different patronage, it is clear that our stake in educational provision is disproportionate to our needs.

One of the concerns we have in this regard is outlined in our policy document of 2007:

> It is sometimes the case that people choose a Catholic school simply because it is the only school available, and not because they wish their children to have a Catholic education. This can cause difficulties for parents who do not share the ethos of a Catholic school. It can also put an unfair financial and administrative burden on the parish. We feel that in such circumstances the Church should not be left with the task of providing for the educational needs of the whole community.[7]

The Church's historical stake in education is changing for many reasons. The question of new schooling arrangements arises and the place of religion within them. This is a question not only for the Church but also for parents and for the State.

ii) New Models of Patronage

The practicalities of the Church adjusting its involvement in Primary Schools to a more realistic and manageable level are

---

7. Irish Catholic Bishops' Conference, *Catholic Primary Schools: A Policy for Provision into the Future*, (Dublin: Veritas, 2007), p. 6.

quite complex. The growth of other sectors helps to achieve a better balance but this growth should not take place in such a way that no provision is made for Catholic schools in newly developing areas, which I believe has happened in some cases. In other situations, where an existing Catholic school is no longer viable as a Catholic school because the Catholic children are now a small minority in the school, the Patron may wish to relinquish ownership of the school. That would be very much a decision for the local Patron and clearly not one which would be taken lightly. It would necessarily involve consultation with the parents, the teachers and the local community all of whom have a stake in the school.

In general, I would say that, faced with the prospect of relinquishing ownership of a Catholic school in favour of another model, Catholic Patrons would favour transferring to something modelled closely on the existing second-level Community School. This would involve the Patron entering into a joint patronage or trustee arrangement with the Department of Education and Skills. Such a joint patronage might even include another religious patron of a different faith or denomination. The resulting school would be genuinely multi-denominational in that it would include all and try to cater for the religious instruction and worship of the different denominations represented in the school. It would also have the advantage from the Church's point of view, over the new Community National School model proposed recently, that the Church would, through the exercise of its joint trusteeship, have an input into the management of the school. This in turn would give it a voice in shaping the ethos of the school and in particular regarding the provision of religious education in the programme.

Having said that I think it is important that I reiterate our position as a Church of intending to maintain a vibrant Catholic primary schools sector in the future. This was stated clearly in our policy document of 2007 already quoted. Paragraph 2.1 of that documents says: 'The Catholic Church is committed to providing Catholic schools to cater for the needs of parents who wish their children to have a Catholic education.'[8]

---

8. Ibid., p. 3.

Keeping The Flame

The Church has a vital role to play in keeping alive, promoting and exemplifying commitment to education as a value in itself. Education in a secular, consumer society is always in danger of becoming a product, a commodity. In the era of the rise and fall of the Celtic Tiger it is difficult to resist the consumer model of education focused primarily on the service of the economy. The emphasis tends to be on competition and there is often a narrow focus on academic and easily measurable results.

The Catholic Church chooses to be a patron in education because of its commitment to the ethos/characteristic spirit that inspires our schools. When we reflect on the ethos that underpins our Catholic schools we are immediately aware that it aspires to provide education and formation that offers hope to the young, that aims to create a community where a sense of belonging is central and the dignity of each person is recognised. While our schools respond to the needs of our modern secular society they '…believe that over-emphasis on competition, a too narrow preoccupation with examinations and specialising at too early an age on highly specific courses are inimical to true education.'[9]

Who could argue against the need for education thus inspired as a contribution to the good of young people and to the common good of society? I will conclude with a rather long quotation from the same paper by Joseph Dunne, which I quoted earlier, and which argues the case for the place of the denominational school in State education provision. He is speaking about the responsibility of politics in relation to the common good. He makes a distinction between two understandings of the common good. He speaks of a 'thin', or 'procedural' notion of the good, by which I think he means a minimalist conception of it, a lowest common denominator, as we say. He contrasts this with 'thick' or 'substantive' notions of the public good that are wide enough to embrace particular traditions in society, for example religious traditions:

---

9. *Vision 08: A Vision for Catholic Education in Ireland*, p. 6

Although education is indeed an inescapably political matter, perhaps we should recognise an important difference between the imperatives that govern politics in the wider sense and those that govern education specifically. Must the school system be treated on all fours with the legal system – in the sense that, just as one set of laws binds indifferently all citizens, so one type of school must indifferently be available to all pupils? An upshot of pluralism at the legislative level is that it commits a society at this level to what has been called a 'thin' notion of the good. While this 'thin' or 'procedural' notion of the public good may be desirable as a constitutional/legal level, ought education be open to 'thick' or 'substantive' goods – substantive enough, in different cases, to embrace particular traditions? Is education as a humanizing activity weakened if engagement with such substantive goods is foreclosed – to the ultimate loss of civil society itself? To provide substantively rich versions of education in this way, it may be noted, would not entail setting aside procedural principles; for the latter would still be necessary in deciding on equitable and non-discriminatory ways of making such provision, and of course the State would still retain considerable regulative powers. The basic assumption, however, would not be that every school must be congenial to all citizens, but rather that, subject to regulations all citizens should have a congenial school convenient to them.[10]

I believe Dunne makes a compelling case for denominational education as a crucial contributor to the common good in a pluralist society. It is my fervent hope as a school Patron that his vision that 'all citizens should have a congenial school convenient to them' will also be the vision that guides our policy makers into the future.

---

10. *From Present to Future: Catholic Education in Ireland for the New Century*, pp. 220-221.

CHAPTER EIGHT

Managing the Catholic Primary School in Contemporary Ireland

Maria Spring

Catholic Education takes place daily in homes, schools and parishes. As a Catholic community in Ireland we have a proud tradition of schooling at primary and post-primary levels. There are over 3000 Catholic primary schools in the Republic of Ireland. These are either parish schools or schools associated with Religious congregations. We have inherited our schools from past generations of families, teachers, clergy and religious who made great personal sacrifices to provide them. Many generations within Catholic families have often been pupils in the same school. These schools are an important part of our local communities. They have shaped the Ireland in which we live today and will continue to shape our Church, our nation and our society as we move into the future.

The Church has provided schools for many centuries and in the major cultures and countries of the world. Thus every Catholic school is part of a network of schools across time and geographical location. Its 'catholicity' means that it is an 'educating community' within the rich tradition of 'educating communities'.

The proper function of the Catholic School as stated by Vatican II is:

> To create for the school community a special atmosphere animated by the Gospel spirit of freedom and charity, to help youth grow according to the new creatures they were made through baptism as they develop their personalities, and finally to order the whole of human culture to the news of salvation so that the knowledge the students gradually acquire of the world, life and man is illuminated by faith (*Gravissimum educationis*, 8).

The characteristic spirit of a Catholic school flows from the values central to the gospel. The educational vision which flows from these values is one which promotes dignity, self-esteem and full development of each person. Such a Catholic educational vision is inclusive and respectful of all and engages with people of all beliefs.

Primary schooling in Ireland is rapidly changing because Irish society itself is rapidly changing. Historically national schools in Ireland were largely denominational and financially assisted by the State grants from public funds. This is a system that has served the needs of families well for many generations. Socio-cultural change, influenced by an increased desire for parents to exercise their right to a free choice of schooling, has resulted in a rapidly changing educational landscape particularly at primary level. New multi-denominational schools are opening and providing parents with some alternatives to the longer established denominational schools. The Catholic Primary School Management Association (CPSMA) is committed to supporting other forms of patronage both existing and new. Bishop Leo O'Reilly in launching the Bishops' document on 'Catholic School Provision into the Future' welcomed the additional model of patronage. However, it must be understood that this is an additional rather than a replacement model. Catholic schools have a unique contribution to make in the task of ensuring that the message of Christ is delivered to and witnessed by our young people.

There is an emerging legal framework for education at national and European levels as well as documentation from Church sources which invite Catholic schools to re-imagine their Catholic identity in a generous and creative way. It is clear that for Catholic schools to continue to serve families in contemporary Ireland, those who manage the school, particularly Boards of Management, must approach the task in an active partnership with all who have a legitimate interest in the education it provides.

Here I would like to focus on the Schedule for Catholic Schools and relate the Schedule to the contemporary challenges facing Catholic denominational primary schools by extrapolating its theological and educational vision in the context of the changing landscape of educational management, educational provision, religious commitment and religious diversity.

The Schedule is an important document for those involved in any way in the life of the Catholic school. It is a public document and must be displayed at the entrance to the school. Not only must it be displayed, it must play an active role in the daily life of the school.

- Parents applying to enrol their child in the school, all staff seeking employment in the school and all who are nominated by the Patron for appointment to the Board must be made aware of the content of the Schedule, helped to understand it, and indicate (in an appropriate way) that they will be respectful of it.

- The Schedule should be considered in the formulation of all school policies. It should be circulated, along with the school's Admission Policy, to all parents applying to enrol their child in the school.

The Church establishes Catholic schools as an act of service to the community and the parents. The Catholic school is a faith school that expresses a set of core values that can be described as human, religious, Christian and Catholic. The values of a religious and Christian ethos are included within the understanding of being 'Catholic'; they are not separate from it. These values define its educational ethos. What really makes a Catholic school different is that it has a religious-Christian-Catholic educational vision, which flows from an understanding of what it means to be human in the light of the Gospel of Jesus Christ. Those who identify with and respect these core values are particularly welcome in a Catholic school. This Catholic ethos is a result of the wisdom gained from the experience of numerous generations of Catholic parents and teachers, parish communities, religious congregations and Church leaders. A Catholic school is one that provides an education based on a tradition of living faith together. Together, the Board, the Principal, and the staff, working with the Patron, the parents and the local parish, model a living human-religious-Christian-Catholic educational tradition to nurture the faith of Catholic pupils in a manner that is welcoming and inclusive of the presence in that Catholic school of pupils committed to other religious traditions.

The Church upholds the principle of a plurality of school systems. A pluralist society respects the right of different religions and cultures to exist within a legal framework within the legal structures of the State. The idea of a 'one size fits all' is not the answer to the needs of a Pluralist Society. Catholic tradition has always emphasised that parents are the primary educators and that the role of the school is to work in partnership with the family. Parents have the right to a free choice of schools in a manner that reflects their religious convictions. Equally the Catholic school has a right to be characterised by a distinctive ethos. Parents must therefore be made aware of the distinctive ethos of the school so that they can make an informed decision to send their child to that school. In practical terms some parents have limited choice. It is for this reason that parents have a constitutional right to withdraw a child from the Catholic Religious Instruction provided by the school and the school has a responsibility to facilitate the parents who wish to provide for a separate religious instruction for their withdrawn child.

The *Code of Canon Law* deals with Catholic education in canons 793-806. The duties, rights and obligations are identified:

- Parents have a right to choose a school which will provide an education in keeping with their own beliefs and values. Catholic parents have the right to choose the school which best promotes the Catholic education of their children (canon 793).
- The Catholic Church claims the right to establish its own schools and to provide for the education of its members (canon 800).
- If there are no schools in which an education is provided that is imbued with a Christian spirit, the diocesan Bishop has the responsibility of ensuring that such schools are established (canon 802).

The aim of the Catholic school is to ensure that the message of Christ is not only taught through the religion programme but that it permeates every aspect of school life. The Catholic school does not just teach about religion but teaches for religion by actively promoting development in faith and does so from the experience of being part of a vibrant faith based educating community. Catholic schools seek to create and develop communities of faith and learning inspired by the teaching of Jesus Christ. Schools strive to provide 'an atmosphere where the gospel message is proclaimed, community in Christ is experienced, service to our brothers and sisters is the norm, and thanksgiving and worship God is cultivated'.

Catholic schools have always welcomed and catered for pupils from other countries and for pupils born in Ireland but whose parents came from different parts of the world and have different ethnic, cultural, and religious backgrounds. These pupils have enriched our schools and in accordance with Rule 69 of the Rules for National Schools provision is made by the Principal, Teachers and the Board of Management for the parents of these pupils to arrange for Religious instruction of these pupils within or outside the school day.

The very essence of a Catholic school is to welcome the Catholic children of the parish and at the same time welcome and assist those students who are not of our faith and who have come as strangers to our country, seeking a new life, to settle into school and be included in the school curriculum and environment. This presents its own challenges to Boards but these new students are an asset to our schools.

Catholic schools respectfully welcome wherever possible, children of other faiths and none. Our Catholic schools are among the most inclusive in Ireland today. *Vision 08* states that 'Catholic education values tolerance and inclusiveness'. Catholic schools are open to children of all denominations. It does not state that a Catholic school is only for Catholic pupils, nor does it state that a Catholic school provides what may be called a 'common' or multi-denominational religious programme open to all religious faiths and none.

The enrolment policy of the school is an important means of implementing Catholic ethos. In the draft template for Admission/Enrolment procedure in Catholic National Schools (*Solas*, April 2008, AGM Special Edition) it is stated at the outset that: 'The school has a commitment to diversity and inclusivity while, at the same time protecting the integrity and Catholic ethos of the school'. It is noteworthy that it is only where the applications for enrolment exceed available spaces that children will be enrolled in accordance with the criteria set out.

The main function of the Board is to manage the school on behalf of the Patron and for the benefit of the students and their parents, and to provide an appropriate education for each student at the school (Education Act 1998, Section 15[1]). The Board in exercising its responsibilities on behalf of the Patron is expected to make the Catholic ethos a living reality in the school and to ensure that ethos related policies are in place.

RESPONDING TO CHALLENGES

Leadership
Research into the ethos of Irish schools indicates that the ethos of many Catholic schools has been diluted. Many Catholic schools are experiencing a displacement in their mission integrity, resulting in an ethos that is overly academic and gives less time to the pupils' pastoral development.

Catholic schools are staffed by good and committed people. Leaders have been described as the custodians of the school ethos. They have a duty to develop and shape the culture in the direction which supports the ethos of the school. However, it is important to recognise that not all who are members of Catholic schools (be they teachers, parents, pupils or members of Boards of Management) are Catholic or active members of the Catholic Church. All school staff, particularly teachers, play and important role in the development of ethos, however, the principal plays a particular role in terms of influencing the ethos of the school. Some of the doctrinal positions that they may be imparting may no longer be a part of their own belief system or reflected in their religious practice.

Effective leadership is vital to Catholic schools; it shapes and influences the entire experience and learning within the school community. Leadership is successful when driven by core values and shared vision and these, in turn, should determine the everyday decision making and ethos of the school. All policies practices and attitudes of the school should be inspired by the Gospel values. Faith and relationship with God are seen as superfluous in an increasingly secularised society. The leadership of a Catholic school is central to ensuring that the beliefs and values are handed on to staff and pupils. The role of the principal in integrating the strengths of the school's historical past with the core values of the present is central. The idea of integrating the past and present seems simple but it is both challenging and critical to the life of the school community. It entails bringing what is best from the past into the future, thus sustaining a vital and rich tradition.

If management is serious about ensuring that Catholic ethos is a living faith reality, I would argue that there is a great need to have a leadership qualification in Catholic Education as a mandatory requirement for appointment to the principalship of a Catholic school. This would assist in faith development both for the principal and the whole school community. It would enable principals to be more confident in exercising and supporting a spiritual leadership in a secular and multicultural reality. If Catholic Education is to mean anything, it must be different to the education offered by other types of schools. This means having a strong vibrant ethos, where faith is expressed by the way that all members of the school community live together.

Looking at a time when clergy are no longer available and the teacher might be the only visible faith presence to the children, it is clear that the challenge of chaplaincy is very real. Many children come to school with little or no awareness of God. The school is now probably the first point of contact and evangelisation for many children from the Catholic communities.

Consideration should also be given to Religious Education as an area of responsibility for a member of the Senior Management/Middle Management Team. The Board should see its work with the Diocesan Advisors for Religious Education as an opportunity to support the development of a quality Religious Education programme in the school. There is perhaps also a need to include a module on Catholic ethos as part of the Religious Education programmes in the Colleges of Education.

Board of Management

Central to the role for the Boards of Management is the maintenance and support of the school as a Catholic school. Patrons ap-
point new Boards of Management every four years. This is always
a very important task for schools and requires a lot of thought. The
necessity for the Board of Management to be familiar with every
aspect of the running of the school is vital. In this context, accountability for the implementation of the 'characteristic spirit' is monitored by the Inspectorate of the Department of Education & Skills.
Patrons will meet with the Board of Management in order to discern the involvement of the board in managing its Catholic ethos
and the implementation of ethos related policies, especially those
related to admission and provision.

A Catholic educational ethos is not just something expressed
on paper or something to be taken for granted. It is to be expressed in the distinctive quality of the daily life of the school
community. The challenge for Boards is to ensure that the Ethos
Statement and ethos related policies are in place and that it can
document a multi-year strategic approach to the development
of a quality Catholic educational ethos. The important point is
that every year the Board, with staff and parents, should set an
achievable ethos-related goal during each academic year and review the achievement of that goal at the end of the year. An internal review of the quality of the school's Catholic ethos should
be carried out each year. This should be documented and the
documents carefully filed.

For instance, the first related goal set by the Board may be the
drawing up of the school's Ethos Statement. At the end of the
year the Board may review the adequacy of the process by
which the statement was drawn up. In another year a Board
may set an ethos related goal of working with the families of relevant pupils and the local parish to put in place a partnership
approach to sacramental preparation.

The necessity for the Board of Management to be familiar
with every aspect of the running of the school is clear. In recent
years a notable feature of the structure of Boards of
Management has been the growing number of lay people who
are being appointed as Chairpersons. CPSMA, in consultation
with the Patrons, will need to continue to plan for and resource

this development. In conjunction with the Patrons, discussion should commence in the twelve months leading up to the establishment of new Boards so as to ensure that suitable persons who could be considered for appointment as Chairpersons and Patrons nominees on Boards and be trained in some aspects of the Constitution and Rules of Procedure of Boards of Management, particularly the section dealing with the Board as a Corporate Body and Catholic ethos. This would create a heightened awareness that the Board of Management is managing a primary school which is a Catholic National School.

This training prior to appointment would enhance the working of the boards and enable them to be more proactive in the provision of Catholic education in a changing world. It would provide greater understanding of their role in managing the Catholic school and of their responsibilities to the Patron under the Education Act 1998.

The Board should see its work with the Diocesan Advisors for Religious Education as an opportunity to support the development of a quality Religious Education programme in the school.

Management has responded positively to several of the challenges. CPSMA and the Mater Dei Institute developed, as a joint initiative, the Wellsprings programme to help Boards of Management for primary schools in their task of understanding and promoting a Catholic educational ethos. This programme provides the theological perspective from which Catholic ethos is explored. The programme complements the wider training for new Boards of Management provided by the Department of Education & Skills. Participation in the Wellspring's programme enabled members of Boards to come to fuller understanding of the many responsibilities, including responsibility to the Catholic ethos of the school.

PARTNERSHIP

School Staff
The Board of Management must also work in an effective partnership with the staff, teachers, special needs assistants, administrative and support staff. On a day to day basis it is the

staff, who express to the pupils and parents a vision of the school as a Catholic school community.

Religious instruction for Catholic pupils means leading the children in an understanding of the liturgy, personal prayer, doctrine and moral education of their family faith. To do anything else is to lessen the idea of religious instruction and is not honest.

Our teachers need support so that they can continue to be living witnesses and so that their identity as Catholic teachers does not become confused, blurred or even suppressed. Opportunities need to be created so that teachers can participate in prayer and worship so as to better understand their role in the faith formation of the pupils.

God is always communicating with us. Therefore it is necessary to find creative ways to enable our teachers to decipher His voice from all the other voices we now have in our lives. In scripture Jesus tells us that, 'I have come that you may have life and have it to the full' (John 10:10). We need to renew our appreciation in our teachers for the potential this fullness offers.

Parish

The Board should promote and develop close links with the parish and the wider community. It is important that the local priest should visit the school regularly. In particular, the Board should encourage the priest of the parish to assist in the preparation of the pupils for the sacraments of Penance, Eucharist and Confirmation and also to involve the school in the liturgical life of the parish. We need to build on former traditions and create new, relevant and contemporary ones to take us into the future.

Diocesan Structures

CPSMA is organised on a diocesan level. There are twenty-six dioceses in the country and twenty-four of them are involved in primary education in the Republic of Ireland. Each diocese has an appointed diocesan education secretary. Currently there are full-time education offices in Dublin, Cork & Ross, Limerick (serving Kilalloe, Limerick and Kerry dioceses) and Tuam. The Diocesan Education Secretary will usually be the link between the Board and the school. As a part of the CPSMA structure, Diocesan Secretaries are an invaluable resource, who provide support and advice locally to their schools. Their role is crucial to ongoing support and training of Boards of Management at local level. The challenge is to provide for fully staffed offices at diocesan/provincial level to work with schools locally to ensure that each school fulfils its functions as set out in the Education Act 1998 and is accountable to the Patron.

The Catholic school cannot be considered separately but must be related to the world of politics, economy, culture and society as a whole. For its part the Catholic school must be firmly resolved to take the new cultural situations in its stride and by its refusal to accept unquestioningly education projects which are merely partial, be an example and stimulus in the forefront of ecclesial community's concern for education (*The Catholic School on the threshold of the Third Millennium*, 16).

Ireland has become a pluralist, multi-cultural and secular society. This means that the Church must recognise that it no longer has a monopoly on education. Catholic education must recognise itself as one player among many. This is an opportunity to rediscover the particularity of Catholic identity and CPSMA needs to be central to this. In February 2005 CPSMA policy stated that 'there is agreement for a new approach that will help Catholic education meet the challenges it now faces.' CPSMA recognises the need to present and explain the values of Catholic schools in everyday life, something that can be difficult in today's Ireland. In this context CPSMA welcomes and supports the establishment of Catholic Education Service. The Catholic Education Service supports Catholic educators in the core activities of learning and teaching, fostering a high quality lifelong learning and the faith development of all learners.

The capacity of management to respond to these challenges will depend on the level and nature of resources – human and natural – which is available to Boards of Management. It will also critically depend on the opportunities for Continuous Professional Development being made available to all Boards.

CHAPTER NINE

Catholic Primary Education: A Parent's Perspective

Ciana Campbell

Normally when I am preparing to speak on a topic the speech or talk follows a certain logic. You would find a beginning, middle and end where a position is stated, explained, supported, where opposition is anticipated and dealt with and where it is neatly drawn together in conclusion. This however cannot be the case here. By its very nature a request for a parent's perspective on Catholic Primary Education invites the personal not the political, the subjective not the sociological and it invites anecdote not overview.

Revealing the personal is not a position with which I find myself very comfortable, ironically given that my professional life has often involved peeling back layers in the lives of others, sometimes with the full permission of the subjects, sometimes, as is often the case in investigative journalism, very definitely not. My reluctance stems partly from the desire to protect my home life but also because once you spend time in the public eye you are held up as an example, for good or ill.

In giving of my perspective, I am conscious that I speak for no one but myself. I cannot speak for others. I am not speaking as a representative of a parent's association or of a Board of Management. This may give you a very limited perspective of how parents feel about Catholic Primary Education in Ireland today but I will let you be the judges of that. Having said that I draw on my experience of being a parent in both Church Of Ireland and Catholic schools and of time spent in Parents' Associations and Boards of Management.

When our eldest daughter was born in August 1991 we lived in Dublin. After about six weeks a neighbour asked if we had put her name down for any schools. My husband and I are not from Dublin but knew that there was often high demand for secondary schools and said that we hadn't but named a few and asked what she thought. She looked at us with some surprise and explained that she was talking about Primary school. I'm from County Mayo and my husband is from Cavan; the idea of a waiting list for Swinford or Killeshandra national schools was not something we had previously encountered. How times have changed! Our neighbour, although a practising Catholic, had enrolled her children in a nearby Church of Ireland school and they were happy with it.

At this stage we were lapsed or even collapsed Catholics and had no plans to baptise our daughter. So, Kildare Place School seemed as good a place as any to start. Our application was well received, the enrolment policy naturally gave preference to those from Church of Ireland families but there would be a place for her when she was five. We were also asked how we felt about her participation in religious education classes and ceremonies. This actually didn't pose a great dilemma because our issues with religion tended to be more with the institutions rather than with the Christian message which still had meaning for us. And so began our journey with religious education in Ireland. Our daughter attended Kildare Place for two years and was very happy there. She participated fully in all aspects of school life and wherever possible we did too.

A desire to return to the West of Ireland brought us to Ennis in 1998 for a trial year, a year where we would see if this was truly what we wanted. The original intention was to live a few miles outside town, near friends, but this was pre the building-boom and there wasn't a house to be rented in the locality. Our plans had included the enrolment of our daughter in the local school but as the summer months went by and the only suitable accommodation available in town we opted to settle in Ennis. This necessitated a quick trawl of the national schools to see if there was a place in first class. Those who know Sr Betty O'Riordan will know why we chose Holy Family School. She extended a great big *fáilte* and we felt at home. Her welcome is perhaps all the more remarkable because we told her the truth about our religious practice. It simply wasn't an issue. We would be accommodated.

Our trial year proved to be a success and now Ennis is our

home. Our two daughters attended Holy Family Junior and Senior
Schools and are now in Coláiste Muire in Ennis. These were all
Mercy schools but Coláiste Muire is now in the care of CEIST.

At this time there was an option for non-denominational education in Ennis as an Educate Together School had just been
founded but we felt that our children would thrive in an established school and were happy with the Christian ethos. The mission statement reads:

> Inspired by the Vision of Catherine McAuley, Holy
> Family School, through a holistic approach, aspires to
> achieve the full potential of each student, with particular
> concern for those who are disadvantaged and marginal-
> ized. Underpinning this is the Catholic ethos based on
> truth, justice, tolerance, respect, self-worth and a sense of
> oneness with the entire Cosmos.

We were very happy with the inclusive nature of Holy
Family which caters to all regardless of their circumstance. The
Junior and Senior schools are both in Band 2 of Deis and that
tells its own tale. Although I am not writing on behalf of other
parents, I do know that what has been our experience of these
schools has been a deciding factor for many others who have
sent their children to them. Obviously, for some this inclusive
approach is seen as a positive while for others it is seen as a negative. I will return to this later in this paper.

In all their time in Holy Family there was only one incident
which set our children apart on religious grounds. It was a very
small matter but worth retelling. Conscious that the attraction of
the white dress and a wonderful party for Holy Communion
would prove hard to resist we arranged for alternatives so as to
ensure they would not see religion simply as an excuse to line
their pockets and party. We encourage discussion and debate in
our house and as they grew older we gave our daughters the option of baptism. Our eldest girl decided that baptism was not for
her and so while her classmates celebrated their communion in
2nd class we had a special family day.

The Parents' Council in Holy Family helps to organise re-
freshments following Holy Communion and they give out little
bags of goodies to the children. Those children who don't make

it back to the school after Mass get their goodies on the follow-ing school day. One parent who was giving out the bags in my daughter's class discovered that Aileen wasn't included and was very upset by the oversight and it was rectified the next day. As I said it was a vey small matter but what left the greatest impression on me was the upset of the Council at their mistake. Not alone did they seek me out to explain what had happened but since then every effort has been made to ensure that no child is excluded. I take great comfort from that.

In our time in Ennis the demographic changes have been enor-mous and now Holy Family Schools have children of many reli-gions and none, although Catholics are still in the majority. At last count there were over thirty nationalities represented. There are probably over sixty children who are not Catholics out of a student population of almost six hundred. From what I have observed, both through the Parents' Council and the Board of Management, the religious mix has not caused any major issues for parents. The schools' Catholic ethos has not been diluted to accommodate other beliefs but respect and tolerance have been shown.

I return briefly to our family's religious journey. As you know, attending a Catholic primary school involves far more than classroom instruction. There are Carol Services, anniver-sary Masses, the celebration of various sacraments and so on. We took part in many of these as you do naturally because your children are taking part. As time went on our daughters opted to become Catholics and they were greatly facilitated in doing so by the school, by the two principals Sr. Betty and Margaret Cooney, by the priests of the parish and by the Mercy Sisters. Our thinking on the matter was influenced by the realisation that the childhood experience of religion can be very special and is of that time. It cannot be recreated for them as adults. We did not feel that we were in a position to deny them that experience. I must stress that there was never an ounce of pressure brought upon them to come to this decision. Naturally, they had ab-sorbed the religious instruction at school but equally they knew of our ambivalence on matters religious. Our daughters, howev-er, know their own minds.

In a small community we are drawn in to religious practice in many ways. Our girls sing, dance and play musical instruments

so I have often found myself sitting in a pew during their re-
hearsals, attending Mass, participating in parish activities only to
be enriched by the experience. Our girls also enjoy the experience
but they have also found great comfort from their religion at
times of pain and sorrow such as recently when their beloved
aunt died. Their lives have been spiritually and emotionally enriched by their religion.

I have often heard people on radio decrying the fact that parents who do not practise are allowed to enrol their children in
Catholic schools. I have heard those in authority in the Church
proposing that those children should not be given the sacraments and I have wondered about the wisdom of these positions. It is not for me to say what is right or wrong and indeed
there is validity in both sides but I do wonder where our journey
would have led us if we had not been welcomed by Sr Betty. I
should add that I'm not suggesting that schools have a proselytising role.

It is interesting to note that on a national scale this welcome
in Catholic schools has been extended to many newcomers. At
an IPPN conference in Killarney that I attended, Ruairi Quinn,
then Labour Party spokesman on Education, acknowledged this
fact. It is also in line with the *Vision 08* statement from the Irish
Catholic Bishops' Conference which states:

> Catholic education values tolerance and inclusiveness. In
> an increasingly multicultural society, Catholic schools
> welcome pupils of other traditions, faiths and none. The
> schools see such diversity as offering opportunities for
> deeper understanding among people holding diverse
> convictions. Such diversity also promotes the common
> good of society as a whole.

Some of my friends in Dublin, whose children attended non-
denominational schools, spoke of their bemusement at how
much more multi-cultural and multi-denominational our girls'
education was when compared to their children's experience.
What had happened in their case was that their well established
schools had enrolment policies that favoured siblings and so
perpetuated a very homogenous student base: mostly white,
middle class and of Irish parentage. This of course is not always

the case but then again I am only offering a personal observation. This experience in Catholic Primary Education also contrasts sharply with what could be described as the upholding of privilege in fee-paying Catholic Second level education in parts of Ireland, particularly Dublin.

I now return to our own story. There is a very active parents' council in Holy Family which provides great support for other parents and lasting friendships are forged over the bubbling Burco. Among its many endeavours, it supports the school and parish in faith formation and in religious practice. The council is also encouraged by the two principals to contribute to the development of school policy and parents are involved in preparation for the sacraments in a caring and meaningful way. There are strong links with the Parish, facilitated no doubt by the fact that the schools are situated right across the road from Ennis Cathedral and the Mercy Sisters also live nearby.

My own involvement with the Parents' Council led to a nomination as parents' representative on the Board of Management and subsequently my appointment as Chairperson. I am now halfway through a second term on the Board and all I can say is that if you ever want to understand primary education serve on a board of management. Others can speak more comprehensively about the role of the boards of management but there are a few brief observations worth making.

One of the issues that needed to be addressed in Ennis was concern over the fair distribution of disadvantage throughout the Catholic primary schools, that every school was meeting the needs of those children who perhaps come with extra needs to the education system ... and this led to a process of engagement for all the parish schools that may yet provide a model for other communities. An education forum was established under the aegis of the Parish Council and this led to a common enrolment policy. St Senan's Education Office, under the leadership of Joe O'Connell, was most helpful throughout this process which I should add is ongoing. The new policy was implemented in 2009/10 and will be kept under review. In referring to all of this I have to be honest and acknowledge that some parents have been reluctant to see their children sharing the classroom with newcomers and those who come from disadvantaged backgrounds.

One moment of this process that will stay with me for a long time was when Bishop Willie Walsh addressed a meeting of the combined Boards and faced the issue of whether to give priority to children from homes where Catholicism is practised. He emphasised that our responsibility was to address the needs of the children, not the behaviour of the parents. Bishop Willie has also been to the fore in apologising for the abuse of children by clergy and for the behaviour of the institutional Church in this regard. This issue has been of great concern to parents and it is very upsetting to see matters unfold as they did recently in the diocese of Cloyne, and the Ryan Report earlier, although I must say that I took great heart from Fr Michael Mernagh's walk of atonement. As a parent it is very important to me that the Catholic Church does not continue to rush to protect those in office at the expense of its most vulnerable members. That has been a cruel double victimisation.

As to the future, I am not so naïve as to believe that children only suffered at the hands of clergy. Most Boards of Management continue to hear of parents who neglect and mistreat their children or of other relatives who abuse children and statistically we know that children are more likely to be abused in their homes. We must ensure that children in our care are protected and that the State, religious institutions and parents are held to account on these matters. The issue of mandatory reporting must be addressed sooner rather than later.

One other area of concern involves the ownership of the schools. In Ireland we have a system based largely on private ownership, where ownership is mostly vested in the Catholic Church. Given the decline in the numbers of religious this naturally raises questions about what happens to the school's ethos and, in some cases, to the physical building, at a time of transition. This will eventually be an issue for schools such as the Holy Family Schools, since it is a Mercy School and parents will be interested to see how it unfolds. The second level Coláiste has already moved into the care of the CEIST and parents were involved in that process. No doubt the same will apply at primary level in due course.

The issue of ownership does concern me, as it did the parents in Seamount College in Kinvara because the prospect of these vital civic facilities being moved or closed perhaps to serve the needs of the religious community as opposed to the student body. It does bring into question issues about planning and provision for education and where that responsibility lies. On the other hand, I don't think that many parents would be happy if all schools were secularised and that Catholic Primary Education became the preserve of those who could afford to pay. This moves us a million miles away from the mission statement that I read earlier that promises social justice.

Another reality that is unfolding came to mind last Sunday as I attended Mass in the Franciscan Friary in Ennis to mark the 800th anniversary of the Order in Ireland. While waiting for Mass to start, my eyes were drawn to the Poor Clare Sisters who were seated nearby. It struck me that the decline in numbers of women joining religious orders means that future generations of Irish children will see very few women in strong positions within the Church. Women exercised significant power and influence through their membership of various religious congregations, particularly in health and education. They were able to develop according to their vision and while this was not without constraints it certainly gave them status in the Church. I know that there will be strong lay women but it is not exactly the same thing. The likelihood is that pupils will still interact with priests but not with religious sisters. This is simply an observation.

As I signalled at the outset, my experience is unique to my family and I am reluctant to draw any general conclusions from it. To get the views of parents and a sense of what they want from a Catholic education for their children and how they see their role in it, it would probably be a good idea to commission research on the subject. Good qualitative and quantitative research should unearth all manner of food of thought. Without such data it is difficult to plan the forward route.

My instinct is that most people will want faith formation in their schools but in an atmosphere of respect for all. Most of us want our children to thrive in school, to grow in ability and confidence and to have a sense of right and wrong. We want to be supported in our parenting efforts and in our role as the primary educators of our children but we do acknowledge that we, too, are on a learning curve and need guidance along the way.

CHAPTER TEN

What is it to be a Learning Society?
Exploring a New Horizon for Catholic Education

David Tuohy

INTRODUCTION

In this paper, I would like to explore the provision of Catholic education as a contribution to the development of a learning society. Firstly, I will explore the concept of the learning society and the forces that contribute to it. Secondly, I will explore approaches to policy development in Irish education and the challenges that exist to develop a learning society, with particular emphasis on the contribution the Church can make to that development. Thirdly, I will speculate briefly on some of the issues for Catholic schools in becoming learning organisations.

THE CONCEPT OF THE LEARNING SOCIETY

Recent decades have seen a major emphasis on the concept of 'learning' as opposed to 'teaching' or even 'knowledge'. The importance of that shift is captured in the words of an American philosopher, Eric Hoffer:

> In a time of drastic change, it is the *learners* who inherit the future. The *learned* usually find themselves beautifully equipped to live in a world that no longer exists. (*Emphasis added*)

The message is that, in the current environment, knowledge often has a short shelf-life, and it is only those who can continually update their knowledge (the learners) who will maintain their position in and contribute to society. The rhetoric promotes 'life-long learning' as a goal of education and for personal development. In the classroom this has resulted in new curricula seeking a different balance between product and process. There is a growing emphasis on active learning methodologies and on assessment for learning techniques to compliment the assessment of learning. Also, in professional development, there is a greater emphasis on the reflective practitioner and on action research.

Organisational theory has seen a similar shift. Since the 1960s there has been a strong focus on the knowledge society. This recognises the increased rate of change in the environment in which organisations operate, mostly due to advances in technology. These bring with them a decrease in the intensity of human involvement in production and an increase in the need for information systems to manage developments. Allied to these developments is the realisation that established, hierarchical systems of organisation are no longer suitable to many systems of management. The hierarchical approach is geared to control and command, with an emphasis on predictability and reproduction. What is required in the new environment of rapid change is the ability to be flexible, to adapt to new situations quickly and efficiently.

The first focus on developing this type of organisation was on the individual. Theorists such as Argyris and Schon promoted single- and double-loop learning whereby members reflected on and learnt from their experiences. There was a parallel focus on the role of the organisation in promoting this, captured by the work on organisational culture of people like Schein, who looked at the way assumptions on how to handle different situations became embedded in organisations. These cultures could either promote or hinder further learning and adaptation.

Peter Senge developed five characteristics of successful learning organisations.

1. *Personal Mastery:* arises from the importance of the individual in any learning process. Unless there is a commitment from individuals to grow and develop, then there is no learning within the organisation. However, individual growth does not necessarily give rise to organisational growth. Drucker observed:

> There is nothing so useless as doing efficiently that which should not be done at all.

In the learning organisation, mastery goes beyond competence and skill. It is based on a continuous process of clarifying what is wanted, and realistically assessing where one is before responding. In the learning organisation, personal mastery is embedded in vision and purpose.

2. *Mental Models:* reflects the way we organize our experiences.

We see what we believe.
We see things not as they are, but as we are.

Mental models are paradigms or patterns of thought created by the mind to organise experience. They are often very useful when confronted with large amounts of data, but they also have the downside that they sometimes filter out that which does not fit with existing patterns. A key to the learning organisation is to reflect critically on the mental models within the organisation, and to develop appropriate and inclusive approaches.

3. *Team Learning:* The importance of teamwork is captured in the phrase:

No one can whistle a symphony. It takes a whole orchestra to play it.

In the complexity of the context of its existence, the learning organisation depends on teamwork, with individuals bringing diverse skills and committing themselves to an agreed outcome. A key for the organisation is the willingness of members to align around the goal of the team. Frequently, this gives rise to demands on leaders to develop team approaches to decision-making. There is an equal need for everyone to develop skills of 'followership', where they play a 'critical' role in the development of the team.

4. *Shared Vision:* results from good teamwork. The vision arises from what individuals have in common. Because of the dynamics of good teamwork, excesses of fragmentation and personal agendas are avoided. The type of vision that is promoted here is not simply a blueprint as to where the organisation should be going. It is more prophetic, reflecting on the messages of the present in the light of the past and the desired future.

A preoccupation with the future not only prevents us from seeing the present as it is, but often prompts us to rearrange the past.

Vision properly developed has a balance of "tenses" – a respect for the past and its traditions, an understanding of the present, and a realistic hope for the future.

5. *Systems Thinking:* is a framework for seeing interrelationships rather than things; to see the forest and the trees. The danger in any organisation is to take simplistic readings of cause-effect relationships and not to understand the complex interaction of personal, institutional and environmental factors, especially when effects only become obvious after long periods of time. A focus on short-term gains and measurement often gives rise to major misunderstandings in organisational growth. A lack of systems thinking often gives rise to fragmentation and negative competition within organisations.

In learning organisations, the result of 'systems thinking' is deep learning. Using the iceberg as an analogy, experience is that portion of the iceberg above the surface – the obvious. However, beneath the surface are questions that analyse, and hypotheses that develop new understandings and mental models. Learning organisations also ask questions that help them manage their experience. Such questions include the challenge 'What is it about our thinking that allows this situation to persist?' When these five characteristics are present in an organisation, then the organisation can be defined as a learning organisation:

> organisations where people continually expand their capacity to create the results they truly desire, where new and expansive patterns of thinking are nurtured, where collective aspiration is set free, and where people are continually learning to see the whole together (Senge 1990).

The focus of the Learning Organisation is on people. The aim is to promote learning in the individual and in the team. The assumption is that if personal and team learning are in place, then effective mental models are brought to bear on situations and realistic visions of the future are developed. This approach to people is empowering. It promotes the ideas of intrinsic motivation, high levels of participation and distributed leadership.

The concepts of the learning organisation can also be applied in larger systems giving rise to the ideal of the learning society. We have seen two examples of such developments in our recent history. In the Catholic Church, the Second Vatican Council gave rise to new ways of the Church thinking about itself. Dulles termed these Models of Church. The contention was that the old institutional model – where Catholic cows ate Catholic grass in Catholic fields – was to give way to more inclusive models. One of these models was based on the experience of community arising from (a) the horizontal dimension of our experience of a common humanity and (b) the vertical dimension of our experience of worship and ritual. A second model was based on the mission of evangelist and herald. In this the Church discovered anew her mission to preach and share the Word of God by direct action, but also by a witness, whereby others say: 'see how they love one another', and thus are prompted to reflect on their lives and to be drawn to Christ.

In Ireland, the celebration of the 150 years since the Famine, gave rise to a number of writings on the change in the Irish psyche, from seeing ourselves as a downtrodden, oppressed people, where our identity was always seen in opposition to others, through to a Celtic Tiger age, where we saw ourselves as having control over our own destiny, giving rise to a new confidence which was seen in entrepreneurship and success at an international level.

Both of these examples involved major shifts in 'Mental Models' or ways of looking at the world. The new insights gave a freedom to see things differently and this gave rise to new possibilities and new actions. However, it would be naïve to suggest that these changes have had universal and consistent application. The ideal of a learning society is just that – an ideal. We still have a long way to go to be a society in which everyone feels at home and the style of democracy gives a sense of participation and contribution to the whole for everyone.

Stephen Covey reflected on the functional and dysfunctional aspects of the Learning Organisation. He identified four elements in individual learning – body, mind, heart and spirit. Each of these elements can promote or distort learning. He then developed four parallel components in organisations – vision, discipline, passion and excellence (Figure 1).

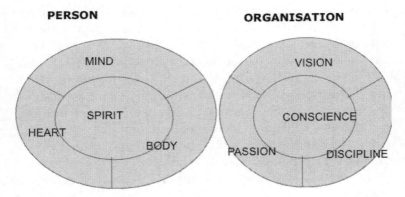

Figure 1. Elements affecting learning in the individual and in the
organisation (Covey, 2004)

Vision gives a clear picture of where the organisation wants
to be. This destination gives focus for action and value. It gives
direction and energy. Lack of vision gives rise to 'drift', 'reactive
decision-making' and 'goal displacement'. It is a case that, with
no destination, every wind is seen as favourable. Decisions are
taken because they 'feel' right. Eventually, the organisation asks:
'How did we end up here?', and the answer is that it left its future to the Fates long ago.

It is also worth noting that a vision that is too narrow, or that
is held in a fundamentalist way, can also be dysfunctional. If we
hold a vision of how the world should be, then we can sometimes tend to see the world in that way. We organise our experience to fit into that vision. We skip over details that contradict or
challenge our vision. We make judgments too early and end up
acting out of prejudice and bias. Vision, to be empowering, must
be open to integrating new information. Only then will the vision come to clearer focus, and enhance direction and energy.

Discipline is the ability to align actions to a desired outcome.
It involves being able to postpone an immediate gratification for
a better future. The dysfunction here can be indulgence, which
seeks immediate gratification with no consideration of the future.
It gives in to the pleasures and distractions of the present moment,
abandoning the present project in order to explore new pathways
– promising that it will get back to the core project again, soon!

Discipline is sometimes confused with being regimented. Regimentation is often the dysfunction of the means to achieving a goal becoming the goal itself. Discipline understood like this can become an obsession, or a guilt for failing to live up to the ideal. The key approach to discipline is to have an appropriate regime linked to the vision of what is to be achieved.

Passion is seen in enthusiasm, excitement and emotional engagement. Without passion, individuals settle for the safety of belonging. They do not move to the higher elements of Maslow's pyramid, overly compliant to the demands of peer-pressure in order to belong. In organisations, this 'safety zone' is experienced in the predictability of tradition rather than the risk that brings growth.

At the other end of the spectrum, passion can give rise to zealotry. The zealot gets carried away with his or her own project, with a single-minded approach that takes no account of other people or other perspectives. The passion of the learning organisation is built on a belief in one's own vision that seeks a dialogue with other people.

Conscience is where individuals and organisations reflect on experience in the light of key themes of justice, truth and fairness. It demands an ethical approach to both the ends and the means of action. Dysfunction gives rise to ego – a self-centred interpretation of events and self-seeking decision making. Ego assumes that the self is all important, and seeks to justify all actions in terms of self-interest. This can mean using very narrow and self-serving criteria for judging success and failing to address wider issues in reflections.

The application of Covey's four areas of vision, discipline, passion and conscience to recent events in Irish society such as the banking crisis and the Ryan Report might be an exercise for another day. There are clearly elements of dysfunction that arose in all four areas.

In seeking to understand the concept of the learning society, we have focused on what promotes the capacity of individuals and teams to learn. This affects the experiences they have, their ability to reflect on these experiences and also their ability to act in new ways out of that reflection. Senge's five characteristics describe an ideal context for the learning society. They explore the link between the commitment of the individual (personal mastery) and the team (team learning) as they seek to promote together (team learning) an approach to systems thinking by continually reflecting on the mental models used in decision-making. Covey's four perspectives make more explicit the components that contribute to the learning organisation with particular emphasis on understanding the functional and dysfunctional parallels in vision, passion, discipline and conscience. In the context of reflecting on these two descriptions of learning organisations, I would now like to explore approaches to education policy in Ireland arising from particular mental models or approaches to system thinking, to view some of the functional and dysfunctional aspects of their development and to trace the implications for schools today.

EDUCATIONAL CHALLENGES IN THE LEARNING SOCIETY

O'Sullivan (2005) has described three paradigms or discourses in the development of Irish educational policy. These paradigms set the vision for society. In understanding the challenges to education to-day, it is important to understand the purpose of policy – the vision behind it – but also to understand the forces that sometimes fragment that policy and make it dysfunctional.

Theocentric or Cultural Paradigm

In this discourse, the aims of education are determined by unchanging Christian principles. Control of education is based in Christian authorities, and policy is formed on the basis of expertise. Education is carried out by trustworthy professionals and the relationship between teacher and students is paternalistic. The school itself is seen as a supportive community. The role of the State is subsidiary to that of the providers.

This paradigm dominated Irish education from 1831 until the late 1960's. The focus was on cultural values expressed through religion (moral outlook and denominational affiliation) combined with nationalism (with a particular emphasis on the Irish language). The approach used in the transmission of values was often custodial, with a strong emphasis on compliance. The current context of cultural transmission is quite different and the challenges are reflected at three levels.

i) *Globalisation*: The development of communications technology and multi-national markets has led to greater ex-
posure and access to ideas, values and practices from
other cultures. On a political front, Ireland has new
European and global alliances that impact on identity.
Through agreements at European Union level, Ireland is
subject to interpretations of laws and directives influenced by other cultures. The arrival of migrants in this
country has challenged the mono-cultural rhetoric we
may have had about ourselves and now forces us to rethink the idea of developing an Irish cultural identity
through education. In general, learning a new language is
seen more as a pragmatic means of communication rather
than an artifact of culture.

ii) *Secularisation*: The religious world view that dominated
Ireland in the nineteenth and early twentieth century no
longer exists. The rejection of hierarchical and compliant
organisational structures as well as 'censorial' and
'closed' approaches to human experiences, and the positive acceptance of liberal philosophies of the person, has
led to very different approaches to religion. These include
outright rejection and antagonism, indifference, a la carte
acceptance of doctrines and rules as well as espousing
personal spirituality as opposed to institutional membership. At the other end of the spectrum, we also see the
growth of fundamentalism in the religious sphere.

iii) *A Scientific World View*: This has come to dominate modern discourse. Science is seen to have answers to major
questions such as the origin of the world, the origin of life
itself and having control over its future development. It is
often proposed that scientific research will solve all problems related to ill-health, even death itself, and that it will
alleviate those situations that give rise to poverty, family
and other natural disasters. This approach excludes the
supernatural.

The Mercantile Paradigm

This paradigm is based on a discourse that gives power to determine the aims of education to the 'clients' or 'consumers', and to give them a voice in the governance of schools. Policy-making is broadly based, using democratic principles. Teaching is carried out on the basis of accountability, and the relationship between teachers and learners is contractual. The school is seen as providing a specific service, and the State operates in a managerial role. This gives rise to three areas of challenge for education:

i)   The human capital approach understands the education system to be at the service of the economy. Key skills are identified that promote and enhance the economy and schools are charged with producing these skills. They provide the infrastructure – the human capital – for economic growth. In this approach, there is a tension between the system needs (the skills required and their distribution) and the personal needs of the participants. A key challenge for education is to maintain the balance between personal growth and development and feeding the economic system with 'disembodied' skills.

ii)   The 'sorting' role of schools is linked to the human capital approach. One approach is to insist that schools assess their students in such a way as to indicate their quality to the system. Thus, the points system ranks students on a 'meritocratic' basis, which allows the system to choose the best for further training, thus capitalising on investment. The challenge for education is to anticipate and deal with the impact of stratification or streaming of individuals on how these individuals see their role in a learning school, and eventually a learning society.

iii) The 'commodification' of qualifications has developed with increased access to education. Educational credentials are the new currency in social advancement. The accumulation of credentials has become a key to social and economic success. The key challenge for education is to ensure that the process of acquisition of these credentials goes beyond a technical or mechanical operation to some form of personal development or transformation.

The Social Paradigm

O'Sullivan explores two areas of development on the social level. The first of these he terms the Human Capital Paradigm, where he examines the effect of market thinking on popular understanding of the role of education and government response (p. 144). This flows from developments discussed under the Merchantile Paradigm. It reflects a changed vision of the role of the human person in society – where persons are valued in terms of their ability to contribute to economic development. From this perspective, attempts to improve the social conditions for individuals are linked to enhancing their contribution to the economy.

The second area of discourse O'Sullivan terms Modernist Discourse, where he discusses the impact of key concepts such as equality, difference, virtue and control on the development of educational policy. In particular, this gives rise to a number of educational challenges.

- Overcoming disadvantage is a key factor in promoting a greater distribution of the rewards of education. Groups not contributing to or benefiting from economic development are seen to lack social or educational capital and interventions are developed to change this. In the past, interventions of this sort were seen as a form of philanthropy, which was often paternalistic in nature and unevenly available. The key challenge is now seen as going beyond providing access to developing the capacity of groups to benefit from the education, thus enhancing both the individual and the system.
- Social Cohesion is a theme that is very much part of the modern political agenda, particularly in the European Union. Despite major projects to alleviate disadvantage in society, statistics show that "class" groups are persistent in their ability to maintain their position in relation to other groups. Schools have been challenged to contribute to social cohesion not just through the curriculum they teach, but also through selection and intake policies. A key challenge for education is the ability of elites to use the system for

their own advantage, distorting the social goals of policy.

- At the core of the social agenda is a humanism based on the confidence that human beings will act selflessly from a belief in the dignity of the human person and a sense of solidarity with one another, with no need for the supernatural. This presents a major challenge, in particular to faith schools.

Each of these paradigms can be said to characterise Irish education policy at different stages – the Cultural Paradigm from the 1850 to the 1960s, the Merchantile from 1960 to the 1990s and the Social from the late twentieth century to this day. However, despite the dominance of one, elements of all three have been present at each stage. The Cultural Paradigm, around religion and Irish identity in nineteenth century provision and the setting up of the State in the early twentieth century, was also closely linked to a desire for the social and economic improvement of the communities in which schools were established. Elements of the three paradigms can be found in many of the debates that surround education at present.

Religion (and education) as a Public or Private Good
In this debate, it is contended that religion, and therefore faith schools, are private, not public, enterprises. Religion is a matter of personal choice and makes no contribution to the public good. As such, faith schools, then, should not be part of public life, and should not be supported as a public (state) enterprise. The opposite side of that debate focuses on the religious experience as part of a core, cultural value system which forms part of a holistic human experience, and therefore deserves support. At the core of this debate is the concept of the human person. Education rhetoric finds inspiration for its activity in the dignity of the person, and seeks to promote that dignity. What is at issue is the source of that dignity. The religious perspective finds that source in God. The secular agenda finds it in a common humanity. The implication of extreme approaches to the separation of Church and State is the contention that these two value systems cannot co-exist, and that the state should favour the secular – an either/or approach – rather than a both/and approach of integration.

Increased Use of Economic Indicators in the Analysis of Education Systems
The development of indicators to measure and compare the performance of education systems is now widespread. Work done, particularly by the OECD and the EU, has had profound effects on national education policy. The goal of the work of these organisations has clearly been to understand the link between education systems and economic growth. This has led to much higher sensitivities about the availability of education and the distribution of its benefits. In Ireland, it has led to greater emphasis on the social dimension of education, and the need to address areas of disadvantage. The downside is that the indicators used have become the only drivers for education policy, and often, the elements of the system not measured have been downgraded.

The Exchange Value of Education
The exchange value of education and the power of elites to manipulate the system for their own benefit remain key issues in Ireland. At second-level, this debate is seen in the focus on fee-paying schools or the ability to use grind schools. At third level, it is often debated in terms of the relative merit of qualifications. This reflects the mass availability of some credentials and the experience of grade inflation. The freedom that some groups have to invest in and reap dividends from the system has meant that there has been relatively little change in the profile of those taking up third level places – the indicator used. The approach to measurement here is firmly based in the economic criteria related to 'standards of living', with little or no focus on 'quality of life' criteria.

To be a Learning Society
In dealing with these questions, what approach can be taken to ensure a learning society? In particular, how does the vision of Catholic education promote this ideal, and what are the challenges for Catholic education? One way of conceptualising the competing contexts of educational policy is to see the values they promote for a different world. Typically, there are three ways of handling complex worlds.

The first is to choose one world to live in and disparage the others. There are some commentators on education that see the only purpose of public education as the promotion of the economy. The goal is seen almost totally as human capital development, and any concession to other positions is a 'sop' to keep people happy. This gives rise to a particular view of selection, streaming, curriculum, assessment and achievement. It places little value on the humanities, seeing their development as the realm of the private, and not part of public schooling. There are others who see education almost totally in terms of a classical Renaissance philosophy, and they resent the intrusion of the economic dimension. For them, the practical and the relevant are related to 'training', which is on a lower plane to that of 'education'. The key dynamic here is the way the mental model is based on giving prominence to one approach, and other approaches are discounted or disparaged.

A second approach is to move chameleon-like between the worlds. In this approach, the individual develops a particular rhetoric when dealing with the different value systems. When talking about the role of religion, culture and language in education they speak about holistic education and the need for students to develop an ethical dimension to their lives. At an economic level, they recognise the importance of both individual and institutional needs in the way the school meets the demands of parents and students, gets good results and places students in prestigious third level courses. They also understand the sociological dynamics at work in school provision, and have views on selection, mainstreaming Special Education, pastoral care and other programmes. The difference in this approach to the first is the willingness to deal with different perspectives. There is a both/and approach, rather than either/or. However, it is like talking to different audiences, and the need is to tell them what they want to hear. The philosophy is fragmented. No connection is seen between the different areas. There is no 'systems thinking' or 'joined-up thinking'. For example, we all recognise the tensions that can arise between curriculum designs and examinations; between teacher education and the reality of schools; between capitation grants and the reality of managing schools. Yet those who work with curriculum design, in setting examinations, in teacher education colleges, as practising teachers, in administering the grant system and in managing schools each believe they are working for the best, and are doing so effectively and efficiently.

The third approach seeks to integrate the issues. The approach to culture and value is seen to inform the economic, and the economic dimension is part of the value system. In considering the organisation of schooling, due attention is paid to the dysfunctional aspects, and attempts are made to deal with inequalities. These attempts are informed by the value systems and the desire for economic development for all parties. The approach here is to include all the issues in the mental model. It is 'both/and', but the method of integration is not just to tolerate different issues and deal with them as problems to be solved. It is to see the issues as opportunities for growth and development – from which real learning develops.

INDIVIDUALISM VS COMMON GOOD
STANDARD OF LIVING VS QUALITY OF LIFE
UTILITARIAN VS TRANSFORMATIVE
EXCLUSIVE VS INCLUSIVE
COMPLIANCE VS FREEDOM
RELIGION VS SPIRITUALITY

Figure 2. Polar tensions that arise in debates on
values and educational outcomes.

Typically, any debate on education gives rise to tensions. Multiple outcomes are possible, and there are often seen as competing or mutually exclusive. Some of these tensions are outlined in Figure 2. It is a worthwhile exercise to trace the arguments used in these debates in terms of the different perspectives outlined above, and to judge how the system has solved the tension – the degree of 'either/or' or 'both/and thinking that has been used. The unpacking of these elements is for another day.

I believe that the Church has a lot to contribute to the development of the learning society. It has a strong philosophy of education that is based on a dialogue between faith and culture. It has promoted, if a little belatedly, the integration of the humanities with science and commerce. It seeks to integrate a strong commitment to the individual's psychological development and the sociological dimension of economic development. In running its own schools, it has focused on both issues of promoting a Church community and on service to the state. However, if it is to make a meaningful contribution to the debate, it must also recognise that it carries baggage from its past. This affects is own contribution, and the way that contribution is viewed by others.

The traditional approach of the Church has been based on the experience of authority. The approach has been deductive. It has assumed a didactic theocentric approach, where the values have been made explicit by an elite, and there has been a strong demand for compliance. The modern world is guided more by the authority of experience. Experiences that are life-giving and empowering become vehicles for exploration of value and for commitment. The approach is one of influence, rather than control. The Church has been slow to learn this lesson. The present developments of setting up a centralised Catholic Education Service with the Catholic Schools Partnership and other bodies must ensure that it does so as a learner, rather than a manager. The approach cannot be that of setting up new hierarchical structures of control, but of promoting networks that empower at a local level. This is not the time to try and recapture the position of the Church in education that characterised the past. The challenges in education, especially in primary education arising from the historical perspective of Church involvement in provision, requires a new approach based on a confidence in the message of the Gospel, and a commitment to helping people discover and live life to the full.

The internal challenges facing the Church in the learning society will centre around:

- *Maintaining a sense of mission*. That means finding a language which helps people discern the impact of the different 'goods' they are being offered through education. The spiritual dimension of their lives must be presented not simply as one option among others, but as an integrating factor that gives meaning and purpose, and leads to a fullness of life.

- *Communicating a vision.* The vision of Catholic education goes beyond a vision of schooling. It seeks to contribute to holistic life-long development. For many people, this vision is a well kept secret. Their imagery is framed in the institutional experiences of the past, some of which were quite horrific. This imagery persists both in the media and in common memory. A key challenge for the future is to show how the vision has changed, to publicise the positive experiences of the current set of students and to make a conscious link to the deepest desires of those coming to Catholic schools.

- *Affirming Catholic schools.* The vision of Catholic education is not just a personal benefit for the individual. Catholic schools also make a valuable contribution to the common good. This is often overlooked in the current debate, where the focus is on past defects, leading to the demand to abolish Church influence in education rather than reform it, or recognise the reforms that have taken place. A key challenge is to name the positive contribution of Catholic schooling as a public good, and to promote awareness of it. Otherwise, Catholic education will be seen as a private option, available only to those who can afford it.

This section has reflected on the development of three paradigms in Irish education. The key challenge for the learning society is to affirm the validity of each of the paradigms in the policy arena, but to hold them in creative balance. Each of the paradigms can find an easy home in the Catholic vision of education, and the Church can contribute fully to the dialogue between these paradigms. However, the Church faces major internal and external challenges in making its voice heard. I have outlined three systemic challenges. They affect Catholic education as a whole. The question now arises as to how this affects the individual school? Can the school be a learning society or a learning school? This is the question I would like to explore in the next section.

The Catholic School as a Learning Society

Our understanding of larger systems comes through our local experience of them. We understand the Church through our experience of the local parish. We understand Catholic education through our experience of the particular Catholic school we attend. We experience the ethos of the Catholic school mainly through our experience of the classroom. Therefore, in promoting the role of Catholic education in the development of the learning society, an important perspective is to reflect on the local implications for individual schools. In this section, I will outline three areas of activity which affect the local school. The reality of these areas are developed in other papers, which witness in no small way to the heroic efforts that are being made to live the reality of the learning society in Catholic primary schools.

Mission

> The Catholic school finds its true justification in the mission of the Church; it is based on an educational philosophy in which faith, culture and life are brought into harmony (*Religious Dimension of Education in a Catholic School*, #34).

The partnership between the Catholic school and the Church is not always easy to develop. The school exists with a lot of competing demands – from the government, from parents, from the local community – as well as from the Church. Dealing with the tension can give rise to three different types of school:

> i) *Education for Catholics:* This approach chooses one world – that of religion – as paramount, and disparages the others. It may be an attempt to define Catholic in a narrow way. It places singular importance on Catholic Religious Education and on Catholic rituals. It insists on the exclusive dominance of this perspective, and may at times see this aspect of the school as more important that education in 'secular' subjects.
>
> ii) *Secular education with Catholic trimmings:* In this link, the school is part of the Catholic franchise. It focuses strongly on the academic and pastoral dimension of the school, and turns at various well set times to Catholic rituals –

sacraments and graduation ceremonies for example. In practice, the school moves chameleon-like between different value systems. In each of the different worlds, it performs quite well. The ceremonies are well constructed, and quite moving. But the values celebrated at these ceremonies do not touch the other areas of school life.

iii) *Catholic education for all:* In this approach, the focus is on people, and linking them in appropriate ways with the values of the gospel. The curriculum helps the students understand the world they live in and to see interconnections between the different areas of knowledge. They are invited to reflect, at an appropriate level, on God's presence in that world through the ongoing action of the Holy Spirit. They are also invited to see God's action in their own story, and to enter into a relationship with him. The key here is an invitation. The approach is deeply respectful of the person, even when they refuse or fail to connect with the invitation, or when they find their response in a different world view.

The ideal of the learning society pushes the Catholic school to the third option, and this is consistent with the models of Church as Community, People of God and as Pilgrim. These models work from the assumption that God is present in all cultures, and that as a pilgrim people we learn from others who are searching in the same way, because we have all been created by the one God. In schools, the focus is on excellence in all aspects of the enterprise. Leaders, teachers, students and parents are engaged in reflecting on the inter-connectedness of school life, where individuals develop as human beings, open to the fullness of cultural experiences, in which they find a living God to whom they relate.

This is the core vision of mission in the Catholic school. Furthering this vision presents a key challenge in the training and supports of Boards of Management if they are to go beyond a technical role of complying with external demands to providing reflective leadership in the school community. Helping them develop the language and tools for theological reflection on their role is a major challenge for the future.

VISION

The main understanding of vision is as a promise, or a desired destination. The vision of the school sets out the ideal of what the school wants to be and how it wants to journey to that ideal. I believe there are four main areas of challenge in developing that vision.

Human destiny and dignity

The Christian approach to education is based on a particular understanding of the human person:

> A human being has a dignity and a greatness exceeding that of all other creatures – a work of God that has been elevated to the supernatural order as a child of God, and therefore having both a divine origin and an eternal destiny which transcends this physical universe. (*Religious Dimension of Education in a Catholic School*, #56)

This view of the person is counter-cultural and competes with very strong forces that see the value of the person in terms of economic productivity, and at times sees personal ethics in relative terms.

Community

The Christian value of community, based on the solidarity of humankind as children of the one God, finds strong echoes among young people, even if the source of that unity is not always understood in that way. However, living out these values in an increasingly multi-cultural society is a new challenge to Irish schools, and one where Catholic schools should be leaders in promoting inclusivity. A more challenging dimension of community is to develop a spirituality of sacrament. I am thinking here of the sacramental experience of meeting God through signs and rituals which is so central to the life of a worshipping community. Many of the traditional signs and symbols of the Church no longer carry meaning for young people. New rituals and symbols need to be developed as a way of helping young people link with the great Christian tradition.

Service

A core element of the understanding of human society is a belief in the ongoing work of the Holy Spirit and the invitation that

God gives to each person to work with him in bringing about the Kingdom. This has major implications in helping students and teachers to see their individual talents as gifts to be used for the benefit of the community. There is a strong pressure in today's world to calculate the cost of commitment in terms of personal gain. Promoting a spirit of service is a countercultural value, but one in which people find great fulfilment.

Focus on the person of Jesus

The gospels show Jesus as a model of human behaviour, and the spiritual view of the person holds that we can develop a personal relationship with him. For many people, God is a 'positive force for good' and young people find it difficult to relate to a God who knows them by name. Developing a vision of how young people can get to know Jesus and develop an appropriate relationship is a key element of the vision of the Catholic school.

These four elements of vision present particular challenges in today's world. However, it would be a mistake for the school to simply focus on finding a new way to express that vision. The destination is only one part of the vision. Vision also involves the capacity of the viewers to see. Without vision, we are blind. A key element of developing vision is healing the blindness of the viewers. This means developing their capacity to experience the Divine, the ability to understand their experiences in the light of the gospel message and the commitment to continually seek meaning and integration of these experiences through reflection. When Covey outlined the vision of a learning organisation, he was very aware of the dysfunctional aspects of organisations that blocked development. In promoting vision, the Church and the school must also be aware of the functional and dysfunctional effects of the forces that impact on realising the vision.

STRATEGY

Traditionally, three approaches have described Church strategy in promoting the gospel message. I would like to illustrate these by three quotations, each followed by a short comment.

i) Witness

Those who practise charity in the Church's name will never seek to impose the Church's faith upon others. They realise that a pure and generous love is the best witness to the God in whom we believe and by whom we are driven to love. A Christian knows when it is time to speak of God and when it is better to say nothing and to let love alone speak (Benedict XVI, 2005).

The first duty of the school is to live its own values. If this is true, then people will say 'See how they love one another', and this begins their search for understanding. However, the problem with witnessing is that people may admire the sign, and not realise to whom it is pointing. This gives rise to the need to explain oneself.

ii) Evangelisation

The obstacles challenging evangelists to-day are not so much the seas or the long distances as the frontiers that, due to a mistaken or superficial vision of God and of the human person, are raised between faith and human knowledge, faith and modern science, faith and the fight for justice. (Benedict XVI, 2008)

The term evangelisation is often confused with proselytising, with images of forced conversions. As understood here, it is helping people to understand their personal and communal histories in terms of God's intervention in history. It is deeply respectful of that history, and sees the Holy Spirit at work in it. The evangelist also learns from those being evangelised. The school is a privileged place to deal with the frontiers mentioned by Benedict.

iii) Discipleship

Part of the overall pedagogy of Catholic schools involves helping pupils to grow in self-understanding and develop a language of prayer with which they can express the search for God which lies at the heart of human lives. Worship of God through prayer and the celebration of liturgy and the sacraments 'the door to the sacred' belongs at the very centre of the Catholic school's life. (*Vision 08*)

Discipleship assumes a level of knowledge and interest in Jesus. The school offers an opportunity for students to grow in discipleship, both through affiliation and by 'growing in knowledge and wisdom'.

The demands of clear witness, respectful evangelisation and ongoing discipleship will be met on many different levels. In a dialogue with culture, there is a psychological and a sociological dimension for the learning school. In partnership with the home, the school focuses on the psychological needs of the child, and develops an ethos of care and personal growth. But there are also sociological dimensions to the impact of the school, and this is an area where we have often not been very reflective. The school seeks to help students find meaningful belonging in society through the curriculum and the social skills that are developed. The schools need to continue to find creative interventions where that sense of belonging is missing or biased.

The school does not have sole responsibility for the faith formation of the student. That takes place in a wider context – in partnership with home and parish. This is the basis of the pastoral strategy of the Church, and focuses on a wider community experience than the school. Linking students with a living parish is a new challenge for both school and parish that goes far beyond preparing students for Holy Communion and Confirmation.

The challenges presented by mission, vision and strategy set the school as a learning organisation. Responding to mission and vision require an engagement with systems thinking and with mental models. The strategies demand teamwork based on a shared vision and personal mastery.

CONCLUSION

This paper has outlined the ideal of the learning society. This ideal includes the growth of the individual, the development of meaningful teams and a shared vision for society. This ideal fits very well with the ideals of Church social teaching and a community based on respect, tolerance and care. The paper has also considered some of the ways that learning can be blocked through individual and organisational dysfunction. Clearly, the Church has reflected both the functional and dysfunctional aspects of the learning society in history.

Education plays a key role in the learning society. The school promotes the learning society, participates in it and embodies it at local level. The paper has traced how education policy in Ireland has sought a balance between three competing but not mutually exclusive paradigms. Because of the historical context in which the education system emerged the Church has contributed in no small way to each of these paradigms. In hindsight, some of that contribution has been positive and constructive. Other contributions have been painfully dysfunctional, and highlight systemic issues for the Church's own functioning as an organisation. Therefore, it faces a major challenge in overcoming the negative elements of the past in order to contribute fruitfully to the ongoing debate on education policy and encouraging the learning society.

The individual school contributes to the learning society when it becomes a learning organisation. For the Catholic primary school, this brings particular challenges with regard to mission, vision and strategy. Other papers in this collection show how the schools approach these challenges from the perspective of systems thinking and understanding their place within that system. This has created new mental models and concepts of team learning. In its patronage and management of the schools, the Church must find ways of continuing to support that development, but in educational interventions, also in forging new links with other areas of pastoral development. In particular, the Church faces challenges by learning from the schools it supports and itself becoming a witness to the ideal of a learning organisation.

References and Further Reading

Argyris, C. (1993) *Knowledge for Action. A guide to overcoming barriers to organisational change*, San Francisco: Jossey Bass.

Argyris, C. and Schön, D. (1974) *Theory in Practice. Increasing professional effectiveness*, San Francisco: Jossey-Bass.

Argyris, C., and Schön, D. (1978) *Organisational learning: A theory of action perspective*, Reading, Mass: Addison Wesley.

Benedict XVI (2005) *Deus Caritas Est*.

Block, P. (1993) *Stewardship. Choosing service over self-interest*, San Francisco: Berrett-Koehler.

Covey, S. (2004) *The 8th Habit: From Effectiveness to Greatness*, London: Simon and Schuster.

Irish Episcopal Conference (2008) *Vision 08* Dublin, Veritas.

O'Sullivan, D. (2006) *Cultural Politics and Irish Education since the 1950s. Policy Paradigms and Power*, Dublin: IPA.

Schein, E. (1992) *Organizational Culture and Leadership*, San Francisco: Jossey-Bass.

Senge, P. (1990) *The Fifth Discipline. The art and practice of the learning organisation*, London: Random House.

Senge, P., Cambron-McCabe, N. Lucas, T., Smith, B., Dutton, J. and Kleiner, A. (2000) *Schools That Learn. A Fifth Discipline Fieldbook for Educators, Parents, and Everyone Who Cares About Education*, New York: Doubleday/Currency.

Tuohy, D. (2009) *School Leadership and Strategic Planning (2nd Edition)*, Dublin: SPELL Training and Development.

Tuohy, D. and Cairns, P. (2000) *Youth 2K*, Dublin: Marino Institute of Education.

Vatican Congregation for Education (1988) *Religious Dimension of Education in a Catholic School*.

Contributors

Ciana Campbell

Ciana Campbell is originally from Swinford, Co. Mayo. Ciana graduated from UCG in 1979 with a B.A. Degree in Psychology. She was a broadcaster with both RTÉ radio and television for many years. She moved to Ennis in 1998 where she provides media consultancy, training and presentation services for a variety of organisations. She is on the organising committee for The Ennis Book Club Festival and she is also chairperson of the Board of Management of Holy Family Senior School. She is married with two daughters.

Kelvin Canavan

Kelvin Canavan is a Marist Brother and has held numerous positions in Catholic Education in the Archdiocese of Sydney. He has been a primary teacher, teacher in charge, inspector of schools and supervisor of Marist Primary Schools in New South Wales, Director of Primary Education and Executive Director of Schools in Sydney. He holds an MSc from Cornell and a Doctorate in Education from the University of San Francisco. He is a member of the Board of Governors of the University of Notre Dame, Australia. He has published extensively on education issues and is in great demand as a speaker on Catholic Education in Australia and internationally.

Roisín Coll

Roisín Coll is a lecturer in the Department of Religious Education within the Faculty of Education at the University of Glasgow. She is also the Postgraduate Convener for the Religious Education department and graduate advisor within the faculty's Graduate School. Roisín previously worked as Classroom Teacher, St. Andrew's Primary School, Bearsden, Glasgow.

Michael Cronin

Michael Cronin is currently a Professor in the Faculty of Humanities and Social Sciences at Dublin City University. He is the Humanities and Social Sciences Secretary of the Royal Irish Academy and Irish Language Literature Advisor to the Arts Council. His publications include: *Transforming Ireland* (2009), *Irish Tourism: Image, Culture and Identity* (2003), *Reinventing Ireland: Culture Society and the Global Economy* (2002).

Eugene Duffy

Eugene Duffy is a priest of the diocese of Achonry and a lecturer in Theology and Religious Studies at Mary Immaculate College, University of Limerick. He has taught at All Hallows College, Dublin, Galway-Mayo Institute of Technology and at NUIG. He was also the Director of the Western Theological Institute, Galway. He is the editor of *Parishes in Transition* (2010).

Dermot A. Lane

Dermot A. Lane is President of Mater Dei Institute of Education, Dublin City University, and Parish Priest of Balally in South Dublin. He has also taught at the Irish School of Ecumenics in Dublin and is a frequent lecturer in the United States. His books include *Christ at the Centre: Selected Issues in Christology* (1990), *Challenges Facing Religious Education in Contemporary Ireland* (2008) and co-editor of *Vatican II Facing the Twenty-first Century: Historical and Theological Perspectives*, (2006).

Tony Lyons

Tony Lyons lectures in the History of Education at Mary Immaculate College, University of Limerick. He has a particular interest in the late eighteenth and early nineteenth centuries. Over the years he has contributed to a variety of publications in journals. He is also external manuscript reviewer in education history for Edwin Mellen Press, New Jersey. His monograph on the education work of Richard Lovell Edgeworth (1744-1817) was published in 2003.

Donal Murray

Donal Murray is Bishop Emeritus of Limerick. Educated at Blackrock College, he studied for the priesthood at Clonliffe College, St. Patrick's College Maynooth and the Angelicum University in Rome, where he was awarded a Doctorate of

Divinity. He has published extensively on issues of ethics, faith and culture and has been a prophetic voice in the Irish Church for several decades.

Leo O'Reilly
Leo O'Reilly is Bishop of Kilmore since 1998. Educated at St Patrick's College, Cavan and Maynooth College. He holds a doctorate from the Gregorian University, Rome. He is a member of the Bishops' Conference Department of Catholic Education and Formation, Chairman of the Bishops' Education Commission and Member of the Bishops' Strategic Task Group for Education.

Maria Spring
Maria Spring is currently Principal of St Clare's Primary School, Harold's Cross, Dublin and Chairperson of CPSMA for the term 2009-2013. She has been a member of the Standing Committee of CPSMA since 1996 and served as Vice Chairperson of the Dublin Council of CPSMA 1993-2001. In addition to this she has long been involved in the designing and the delivering of training and workshops to Boards of Management.

David Tuohy
David Tuohy is a Jesuit priest. He now works as an Education Consultant specialising in leadership support and development and strategic planning. Currently he is the project director for Le Chéile, a new Trust being set up by twelve religious congregations for their schools. He is also the academic advisor to the School Development Planning Initiative. He has worked in the US, Australia and East Africa. He has taught in both UCD and NUI, Galway. He has published widely in the area of teacher and leader development.